ordinary

Harnessing the Power of Or in Everyday Moments

Corrin Spiegel

ISBN: 978-1-972328-24-8
ISBN: 978-1-972328-18-7 (ebook)

Dedication

With gratitude to Kruppy, and for every friend who reads the drafts.

Table of Contents

Finding the "or" in Ordinary i
an introduction

1 **Alone or Known** 1
the fortress that locks you in

2 **Avoid or Feel** 13
the stillness that won't stay silent

3 **Blame or Build** 25
the grievance that consumes you

4 **Chase or Content** 37
the treadmill that goes nowhere

5 **Control or Surrender** 49
the grip that gives nothing back

6 **Defend or Understand** 62
the argument that wins nothing

7 **Envy or Admire** 74
the mirror that you distort

8 **Judgment or Curiosity** 86
the gavel that silences wonder

9 **Lessen or Lesson** 99
the teacher that terrifies you

10 **Perfect or Progress** 111
the fantasy that steals your reality

11 **Perform or Reveal** 122
the mask that everyone believes

12 **Presence or Distraction** 135
the here that keeps disappearing

13 **Reaction or Response** 147
the split second that changes everything

14 **Resentment or Release** 159
the story that won't let go

15 **Someday or Today** 171
the life that you keep postponing

16 **Speak or Listen** 182
the pattern that talks for you

17 **Story or Truth** 194
the fiction that feels like reality

18 **Worry or Wonder** 206
the rehearsal that steals the show

Notes 219

the most powerful patterns are created in the most ordinary of moments

Finding the "or" in Ordinary

an introduction

Most of life happens in moments so small we forget they matter. The quick thought you have while brushing your teeth. The way your chest tightens when someone uses a familiar tone. The quiet decision to push through or pause for a breath. None of these moments look life-changing, which is exactly why they slip past without a second thought. But the truth is that ordinary days are filled with quiet crossroads that shape how you move, how you relate, and who you become. We imagine the big events define us, yet it is the smallest, most unremarkable ones that leave the deepest imprint over time.

I didn't begin contemplating the power of ordinary because I was seeking wisdom. I started because chasing extraordinary had turned my life into something unrecognizable. For more than two decades I had been relentless in the pursuit of the next big thing. Promotions. Cross-country moves. Degrees and certifications. All the achievements that are supposed to make life feel as impressive on the inside as it looks on paper. It worked. Until it didn't. A series of extraordinary events pushed me to the edge, and suddenly I found myself living in a version of my life I didn't recognize. I kept picturing that movie scene where someone clears a table in one sweeping motion, everything crashing to the floor. That was me, metaphorically, staring at the mess and thinking, now what?

There came a moment when the performance of holding everything together became impossible. I found myself weighing my own integrity against maintaining the habit of choosing what made things easier for everyone else. There is a breaking point in that kind of pattern, and I found mine. What followed was a long and necessary spin through the angry stage of the grief cycle. I was not graceful. I was not enlightened. I was simply a person standing inside the wreckage of choices that had become unsustainable. Nothing about that season made me feel stronger, but it did strip away any illusions I had about where real transformation begins.

The shift that came next didn't arrive through insight or strategy. It arrived on an ordinary Tuesday while I was walking my dog along the same stretch of sidewalk where months earlier I had come undone. I remember realizing, with a kind of quiet surprise, that I felt happy. It had been a long time since happiness felt possible. My circumstances had not changed. My life was still in pieces. Yet something in that moment felt steady and true. Nearly a year later, on that same sidewalk with the same dog, I felt joy for the first time in what felt like forever. Not the loud kind. The honest kind. That was the moment I understood the power of ordinary, and it's when I began researching this book.

That is the foundation of this work. I survived. I rested. I learned. And I chose ordinary because it was the only place my life began to make sense again. Ordinary moments saved me long before I understood why. They showed me that the only real control I ever had was in the tiny choices I was making without noticing. Once I stopped looking for transformation in the spectacular and started paying attention to the subtle, my life began to feel different, even though nothing around me had changed.

Every ordinary moment holds an *or*. A quiet hinge asking which direction you will take. Judgment or curiosity. Avoiding or feeling. Performing or being honest. These are not dramatic battles. They are small invitations that appear dozens of times every day. Most people move through these tiny crossroads on autopilot, unaware that anything is being chosen at all. Yet these micro choices create the texture of your life far more than the events you label extraordinary. When you begin to see the *or* inside these moments, you also begin to reclaim the agency you have always had.

You will not find rigid steps or a linear journey in these pages. The chapters in this book are organized alphabetically on purpose because life doesn't hand us experiences in any particular order. Some days you need the tenderness of one chapter. Some days you need the clarity of another. Some days, you reach for the thing you do not want but know you need. Think of it like a recipe book. You choose what fits the moment, not what belongs on someone else's timeline. You can open this book anywhere, and it will meet you exactly where you are.

Each chapter is built on similar scaffolding, so the structure remains familiar as you move through the dualities. It begins with a story. You will meet someone navigating an ordinary struggle that feels anything but ordinary in the moment.

From there, the chapter explores what is shaping the response, drawing on research to give language to experiences many people recognize but rarely name. These sections examine why certain perspectives feel easier, and how those defaults influence behavior over time. The focus then returns to daily life, where these hinge moments show up in small, repeatable ways, often without notice. A set of practice exercises follows, creating opportunities to try different ways of responding. The chapter closes by returning to the story, revealing how the *or* becomes a choice worth making.

It's also important to note that understanding often arrives in the body long before the mind knows what to do with it. A sentence lands heavily. A memory surfaces. A familiar discomfort rises. These moments are not warnings to slow down or stop. They are signals pointing toward something that wants attention. Let them land without rushing to interpret them. Growth is rarely linear. It spirals. You understand something one week and forget it the next. You try, you fall back, and you try again. This rhythm is not failure, it's how real change actually happens.

You don't need to rebuild your life to feel whole again. You don't need to wait for clarity or confidence. The power you are looking for already exists inside the smallest moments of your day. Once you start noticing the *or* in ordinary moments, your life begins to feel different even when the circumstances remain exactly the same. Perspective becomes the shift. Presence becomes the anchor. Choice becomes the quiet power that steadies everything else.

The work begins here, right where you are. You don't need to feel ready. You only need to be willing to notice the next ordinary moment and the *or* inside it.

That is enough to begin.

1

Alone or Known

the fortress that locks you in

The notification lit up Tyler's second monitor at 11:47 p.m., breaking the rhythm of code that made perfect sense because it never asked how he was doing. "Beach house this weekend! Can't believe it's been 10 years since graduation. Everyone's confirmed except you. Come on Tyler, we miss you!!" Jake's message glowed against the darkness of Tyler's downtown loft, where floor-to-ceiling windows framed a city full of people while he sat alone, exactly as he had designed his life. At 32, Tyler had executed his post-graduation plan with surgical precision. Corner office at a tech startup where his architecture decisions moved millions in market cap. An algorithmic trading side hustle that outperformed his six-figure salary. A LinkedIn profile so polished that old classmates sent messages he trained himself to answer three days later with "Thanks, slammed but grateful." Every surface in his apartment gleamed, every detail accounted for. It was a space built for one, perfectly suited to a man who had learned to need no one.

The beach house invitation made his chest tighten in a way no achievement ever had. Ten years since college. Ten years since he had lived with five guys who knew him when he was broke and struggling. Who had seen him cry over his parents' divorce at 2 a.m. Who had stayed up all night helping him prep for exams while eating terrible pizza. They knew the version of

Tyler that existed before he built walls so sophisticated they looked like achievement. His fingers hovered over the keyboard, typing excuses with the same efficiency he used for declining meetings. "Big project deadline." Delete. "Family thing." Delete. "Can't get away from work." That one was technically true because he had made work his identity to avoid this precise recognition.

Another message appeared, this one from Devon. "Tyler, real talk. We're worried about you, man. You've been MIA for two years. Just come for one night. Please." Tyler's hands froze. Worried. They were worried about him. The guy with everything figured out. Who responded to life updates with perfectly calibrated congratulations that revealed nothing about himself because there was nothing to reveal except work and more work and the steadily expanding emptiness where his actual life used to be. He looked around his apartment at 11:53 p.m. Not a dish in the sink. Not a photo on the wall. Not a single trace that he mattered to anyone or that anyone mattered to him. He had 5,874 LinkedIn connections and could not remember the last time he had called someone just to talk. His calendar was full of networking events and strategic coffee meetings, but didn't contain plans with actual friends. No one would notice if he disappeared except his direct reports, wondering why their Slack messages went unanswered.

His thumb hovered over the keyboard. The beach house was three hours away. His weekend was empty except for the work he had invented to fill it. He could type another polished excuse about quarterly targets and initiatives, maintaining the fortress he had spent a decade building. Or he could risk letting them see the person he had become. Someone who had traded genuine connection for achievement. Someone who responded to "we miss you" with meeting decline templates. Someone who was isolated by loneliness while everyone admired his success. This was not about a weekend trip. It was about whether he would spend the next ten years becoming even more successful and even more alone. Or risk discovering if the version of himself that could connect with people still existed under all the optimization, self-sufficiency, and strategic distance he had performed so convincingly that even he believed it was strength.

Why Your Choice Matters

The walls you built were supposed to protect you. Instead, they're keeping you alone. The conversations you keep light and pleasant to avoid revealing that you're struggling. The busy schedule that somehow never has space for the friend who wants to grab coffee. The self-sufficiency you've perfected so thoroughly that asking for help feels like admitting defeat. You've decorated your isolation with achievements, hobbies, and curated independence so beautifully that even you sometimes forget you're alone. This feels like strength. This feels like what intelligent people do after learning that humans are unreliable, that vulnerability leads to disappointment, and that the safest way to live is needing nothing from anyone.

But protecting yourself this way comes at a cost. By keeping pain out, you're also keeping everything worth living for from getting in. The kind of hurt that creeps in while everyone admires how well you're doing. Robert Waldinger, a psychiatrist and director of the Harvard Study of Adult Development, oversees one of the longest-running studies on human happiness, which has followed the same people for over eighty years.[1] The study's findings cut through every excuse you've made for isolation. People who maintain close relationships live longer, healthier, and happier lives than people who don't. Not successful people. Not wealthy people. Not accomplished people. Connected people. You've felt it in the silence of Sunday afternoons when everyone else seems to have plans. In the moments after a big achievement, when you realize you don't know who to call. In the creeping suspicion that if you disappeared tomorrow, people would miss your contributions more than they'd miss you.

You've become so skilled at surface-level connection that you can spend an entire evening with friends and come home feeling more alone than when you left. You can have fifty people at your birthday party and feel like nobody truly knows you. You can achieve your biggest professional breakthrough, only to realize there is no one to call who would understand why it matters. Being known works on a completely different premise. Being seen, really seen, with all your mess and fear and beauty, is worth the risk of being hurt. True connection isn't about avoiding disappointment, it's about choosing people who make the risk worthwhile. The alternative to risking hurt isn't safety. It's slow disappearance. Choosing to be known instead of remaining alone is choosing to be alive in a way that truly matters.

Why We Build Walls Instead of Bridges

Think about the last time someone asked "How are you?" and you said "Fine" while your world was falling apart. That automatic deflection didn't come out of nowhere. It came from an experience, maybe many years ago, maybe yesterday, when you opened up and it didn't go well. Maybe you cried in front of someone, and they looked uncomfortable. Maybe you asked for help and got judgment instead of support. Maybe you loved someone deeply, and they left anyway. Your brain took notes. It created a new policy. Don't do that again. Stay safe. Stay closed. Stay in control.

This makes sense. Your nervous system learned to protect you from repeating experiences that caused pain. When you touch a hot stove, you learn not to touch hot stoves. When vulnerability leads to rejection, you learn not to be vulnerable. John Bowlby, a psychologist and primary architect of attachment theory, conducted research on attachment that revealed how early relationship experiences create internal working models about whether others are safe, whether your needs will be met, and whether showing your true self leads to acceptance or abandonment.[2] Your brain can't tell the difference between a dangerous person and your own fear. It treats all emotional risk the same way, building barriers that keep out not only the people who might hurt you, but also the people who might heal you, celebrate you, or simply sit with you in your actual reality instead of your performed one.

The digital age has turned this protective instinct into something far more insidious. You can maintain hundreds of connections through texts, likes, and comments while never risking the vulnerability of letting anyone see you on a hard day. You can curate your life into a highlight reel that gets applause, while your real life, the one with doubts and fears and late-night anxiety, remains completely hidden. The culture of independence tells you this isn't isolation, it's evolution. That needing no one is strength. That handling everything alone is maturity. So you keep your struggles private, your achievements modest, and your needs invisible. You become someone people admire, but never someone people actually know. The most devastating part isn't that you're lonely, it's that you've convinced yourself you're not. You have friends, family, and colleagues. But when something real happens, when you get scary news or fail at something important, you don't call anyone. Letting someone into your actual experience feels like the whole structure giving way.

Unlocking the Door

Being known requires something that feels impossible until you do it. The courage to let someone see you on a day when you're not okay. Not a dramatic confession or crisis dumping, just honest sharing of your actual experience with someone who's earned the privilege of knowing you. Sue Johnson, a clinical psychologist and creator of Emotionally Focused Therapy (EFT), has spent decades studying how adult love relationships are shaped by emotional bonding and secure attachment.[3] Her research on emotional connection reveals that the relationships that fulfill us aren't built on finding perfect people. They're built on learning to be imperfect with the right people. Her work with thousands of couples and families shows that connection happens in moments of risk, when someone reveals their real struggle and another person responds with presence rather than judgment. You don't need to broadcast your struggles to everyone, but you do need to share them with someone. You don't need to be vulnerable with the whole world, but you do need to be real with a few people who matter.

When Tyler finally typed "I'll be there," it felt like jumping off a cliff. The drive to the beach house took three hours, but passed in a blur of mounting panic. What would he say? How would he explain two years of calculated distance? By the time he pulled up, his hands were shaking so hard he sat gripping the steering wheel for almost ten minutes. Jake appeared in the doorway and waved. Tyler couldn't hide anymore, so he finally got out of the car. That night around the fire pit, Tyler felt his chest tighten every time the conversation drifted toward something deeper. But he was still performing, even here, with people who had once known him completely. The old Tyler would have maintained that performance all weekend, left Sunday afternoon with everyone thinking he was fine, and returned home exactly as he arrived.

Instead, when Jake asked, "So what's really going on with you, man?" Tyler opened his mouth to deliver his polished deflection and stopped. He looked at five faces watching him, and what he saw wasn't judgment. It was hope. He took a breath and said the truest thing he'd said to anyone in two years. "I don't know how to do this anymore. Be real with people. I've spent so long building this perfect life that I forgot to let anyone into it." The silence that followed wasn't uncomfortable. It was relief. Devon laughed and said, "Man, we thought you'd become too successful to need us." Tyler shook his head, eyes blurring. "I became too afraid."

When Both Options Serve the Moment

Sometimes withdrawal isn't isolation, it's restoration. When you're processing grief or recharging your energy, alone time serves you. The difference lies in direction. Restorative solitude prepares you to be known more fully. It fills you up so you have more to give when you let someone in. You emerge ready to be seen. Defensive isolation does the opposite. It makes being known feel more dangerous each time. You withdraw because people feel threatening, not because you need restoration. You emerge feeling more disconnected, more convinced that remaining alone is safer than being seen.

The test is simpler than it looks. Does your time alone prepare you to be known, or does it make staying hidden feel reasonable? Does it restore you for connection, or reinforce the distance you already keep? Solitude that leaves you steadier and more available is serving you. Solitude that leaves you more convinced you don't need anyone is quietly narrowing your life. Not everyone is safe to be known. Discernment is not cynicism. Being known does not mean indiscriminate openness or emotional exposure without care. It means choosing a small number of people who have shown, over time, that they can hold your truth without judgment, without using it against you, without making your vulnerability something they need to manage. The alternative to being known by safe people is not protection. It is remaining alone, even when you are surrounded.

Alone serves when it's temporary and purposeful. When you need space to process difficult emotions. When creative work demands focused solitude. When you're healing from something that requires time alone before you're ready to let others in. Known serves when you're ready to let someone into your actual experience, not just a polished version of it. When you need support you genuinely can't provide yourself. When celebration or grief needs to be witnessed by someone who knows your story to feel real. When your struggles have become so heavy that carrying them alone is crushing you. The meta-skill isn't balancing alone and known, it's daring to be seen as you are, and trusting that being known will change you in ways staying hidden never could.

Where This Choice Shows Up Every Day

Professional Moments. You achieve something meaningful but downplay it in emails and texts. Alone minimizes the accomplishment to avoid seeming boastful, keeping the win private and unwitnessed. Known calls someone who understands what this cost you and shares the full story, letting them celebrate with you. The achievement becomes real because someone witnessed not just the outcome but the work it took to get there.

Personal Struggles. The doctor calls with concerning test results and you carry the fear alone for days. Alone holds the weight in silence, mistaking endurance for strength. Known sends a message that feels impossible to type, letting someone know you are scared. The fear does not disappear, but it becomes bearable because it is shared, and asking for support no longer feels like a failure.

Everyday Moments. Friends invite you to dinner and you immediately start planning exit routes. Alone declines or shows up guarded, keeping conversation on the surface. Known says yes without scripting an escape, and when the moment turns personal, offers something real instead of a practiced deflection. The evening ends differently than you expected, not because it was dramatic, but because you were actually there.

When Others Reach Out. A colleague mentions they are struggling and pauses longer than usual, hoping someone will notice. Alone offers a quick comment that sounds rough before steering the conversation back to work. Known says it sounds hard, suggests grabbing coffee, then listens without trying to fix it. You notice something quiet shift as the conversation ends. The walls you thought were protecting you feel a little less necessary.

Celebration and Crisis. Something big happens and you find yourself alone at midnight with news that feels too heavy to carry. Alone posts a vague update and waits for polite emojis from people who do not really know you. Known calls the person who has earned access to your real story and shares what it actually means. The moment does not become easier, but it no longer has to be carried alone.

Practice Exercises: Opening the Door

Being known doesn't require dramatic confessions or perfect timing. It happens through small choices to let someone see what you usually keep private. These practices create opportunities to notice what shifts when you stop performing safety and allow yourself to be met.

The One-Person Experiment. Choose one person who has earned the right to hear something real. Share a truth you usually keep private. A fear, a hope, a disappointment. Pay attention to what happens in your body as you speak. Does your chest tighten or do your shoulders drop? Does the catastrophe you imagined actually unfold, or does being seen clearly bring an unexpected sense of ease?

The "How I'm Really Doing" Practice. For one week, answer "How are you?" with something true instead of something safe. Not a performance, not a complaint, just honesty. "I'm behind and overwhelmed." "I've been missing meaningful conversation." Then observe. Do people pull away, or lean in? You may discover that authenticity invites connection more reliably than perfection ever has.

The Celebration Invitation. The next time something goes well, let someone see what it means, not just what happened. Instead of sharing only the outcome, include the context you usually edit out. The doubt that preceded it. The effort it required. The relief that followed. Let someone witness your experience rather than a headline. Learning to be known includes allowing your success to be seen as part of your real life, not as something separate from it.

The Request Experiment. Ask for help in a way that costs you a little pride. Not a small favor you could easily manage yourself, but something that requires another person's attention or perspective. Let the request be simple and unpolished. Notice the urge to explain, justify, or soften it. Make the request and stay with the exposure of having asked.

The Presence Test. Spend unstructured time with someone you trust. No tasks, no distractions, no screens. Walk, sit, talk, or stay quiet together. See what surfaces when there's nothing to hide behind. You may discover that the door to being known doesn't open through grand confessions, but through simple, undistracted presence.

The Life Waiting Beyond Your Walls

Three years after that beach house weekend, Tyler stood at Devon's second wedding as best man. In his toast, he told the truth about those years he'd vanished. "I thought success meant not needing anyone. Turns out, success means having people who know you well enough to celebrate when things go right and sit with you when they don't." The guests laughed and cried. Later, Devon pulled him aside. "That toast wasn't just for us, was it?" Tyler nodded. He'd needed to say it. More than that, he'd needed people who could hear what he was really saying. His apartment still had floor-to-ceiling windows, but now the walls held photos. His calendar was still filled with meetings, but also included Tuesday dinners with Jake, and a monthly poker night with the beach house crew. His career hadn't suffered from being more available. People came to him with what actually mattered.

When his father died eight months earlier, he didn't sit alone in the dark. He called Devon at 2 a.m. and cried, something the old Tyler would have called weakness. The evolved Tyler knew it was the only way to stay connected. Every time you choose to be known instead of remaining alone, you choose what Tyler chose. To let yourself matter to someone. That choice determines whether you'll be admired from a distance or loved up close, whether your achievements feel hollow or whole. Relationships deepen because they're built on truth, not performance. Struggles become bearable because you no longer carry them alone.

You develop what psychologists call earned security, the ability to trust connection despite past hurt. Isolation erodes the body and the mind. Connection heals them both. Vulnerability isn't weakness opening you to harm, it's courage opening you to life. When you keep choosing connection, you learn what every wall has been hiding. Being hurt by someone you let in is painful, but living behind walls no one can reach is its own kind of disappearance. Asking for help isn't failure. It's how humans were built to be known, and through that knowing, to belong. Your willingness to be seen becomes the foundation for every meaningful moment that follows. The celebration that feels genuine. The crisis that doesn't crush you. The ordinary day that finally feels alive.

2

Avoid or Feel

the stillness that won't stay silent

Rebecca's phone died at 4:42 p.m. on a Tuesday, and that's when everything she'd been running from for thirty-eight years finally caught up to her. She'd just settled into her car in the parking garage, checking one last email before the drive home, when the low battery warning flashed and the screen went black. Her charger was at home, still forty minutes away through rush hour traffic. She stared at the dark screen for a moment, then started the car and reached for the radio. The pop station was too cheerful. NPR felt too heavy. The classic rock station made her want to scream. She jabbed at buttons, scrolling through stations, but everything felt wrong. Too loud. Too much. Like noise pressing against something already screaming inside her head. She turned the volume to zero. Just her, alone in her car for the next forty minutes, with nothing between her and the feelings she'd been outrunning since she was old enough to understand that staying busy meant not having to feel anything difficult.

Three months ago, she'd held Cooper while the vet administered the injection. Her golden retriever of twelve years, the dog who'd greeted her at the door through almost every loss she'd ever outrun as an adult. She'd felt Cooper's heartbeat slow beneath her palm, watched his eyes go peaceful, and then drove straight to the office because she had a presentation at two.

Everyone had told her how strong she was, how well she was handling it. Strong meant not falling apart, meant staying functional. What they didn't see was the cost. How she hadn't stopped moving in three months. Waking up at 5 a.m. for emails before the gym. Scheduling meetings through lunch. Saying yes to every project and happy hour. Falling asleep with her laptop open and podcasts playing because silence felt like drowning. How she'd donated Cooper's things within a week while on a conference call. How she'd deleted his photos because seeing them hurt, and she'd learned decades ago that hurt wasn't something you wanted to feel, so it became something you ran from.

The divorce five years ago? Started dating three weeks later, joined two non-profit boards, signed up for a marathon. Her father's death eight years ago? Perfect funeral, back to work the next week, every evening filled with obligations. Never cried. Never processed. Even as a kid, when her parents fought, she would lock herself in her room with homework and books, getting perfect grades instead of feeling afraid. She'd been practicing this her whole life. When something hurts, start moving. When something scares you, get busy. When something threatens to overwhelm you, find seventeen tasks that you can do instead. But now, sitting in traffic with a dead phone and nowhere to hide, Rebecca felt something she'd been too busy to notice. Her entire body was shaking. Her hands trembled on the steering wheel. Her chest felt crushed. Every muscle was tensed against something that had been building for decades.

The car behind her honked. Traffic had moved forward. She hadn't noticed. Rebecca pulled into a gas station parking lot because she couldn't see the road through the tears anymore. She sat there sobbing in a way she hadn't allowed herself to since childhood. Ugly, gasping, full-body crying that felt like it might split her open. Not just grief for Cooper, but for her father, for her failed marriage, for every loss and hurt and disappointment she'd been too efficient to feel. Decades of unfelt emotion came pouring out in waves that wouldn't stop. She'd been so proud of how well she handled things. How strong she was. How she never fell apart. Except she'd never handled anything. She'd just kept moving fast enough that nothing could catch her.

And now, alone in her car with no escape and nowhere left to run, Rebecca faced a choice she'd been making unconsciously every day since she was a child. She could restart her car, drive home, plug in her phone, and immediately fill the silence with something that would push these feelings back down. Or she could finally stop running. The difference wasn't about whether the feelings would eventually fade. It was about recognizing that avoided emotions don't disappear, they just run your life from the shadows.

Why Your Choice Matters

The feelings you avoid still guide your behavior. They just do it from places you rarely notice. Something stirs beneath the surface. Grief, loneliness, anxiety, or that hollow ache you can't quite name. Before awareness catches up, you're already moving. Your hand finds your phone, your mind invents new tasks, or your body reaches for distraction. You turn toward anything that softens the sharp edge of what you don't want to feel. It seems automatic, like a reflex beyond your control. But that sense of inevitability is the habit itself. Avoidance becomes so practiced that it no longer feels like something you do. It starts feeling like who you are.

Unfelt emotions don't disappear. They accumulate. Like unopened mail piling up on the counter, each envelope demanding attention you keep postponing. Tonight's drink might mute the ache of loneliness, but it promises the same ache tomorrow. Work that distracts from grief doesn't heal the loss, it adds exhaustion to sorrow. The constant motion that keeps anxiety away eventually makes it your companion, always just behind you, no matter how far you try to run. Susan David, a psychologist at Harvard Medical School and originator of the concept of emotional agility, has spent years studying how our attempts to control or avoid difficult feelings often backfire and keep us stuck instead of free.[4] Her research reveals what happens during this accumulation. The feelings you refuse to face don't dissolve. They reappear as restlessness that never settles. Tension in your shoulders, conflict across relationships, habits that soothe briefly but expand their hold. What begins as self-protection turns into limitation. You are not avoiding the emotion itself but the imagined catastrophe of feeling it.

The calculation is understandable. You believe this feeling is too consuming to face directly. Better to stay busy than risk being overwhelmed. The grief you think will shatter you might ache fiercely and then soften. The anxiety you outrun might actually reveal what needs care. The loneliness you deny might be the doorway to genuine connection. The emotions you fear rarely destroy you, but the avoidance of them will. What you resist exaggerates itself. What you face begins to integrate. Emotional acceptance isn't indulgence, it's the capacity to feel without collapsing, to allow discomfort without surrendering to it. When you practice this, stress becomes more manageable and satisfaction becomes more accessible. The emotions you once feared pass through instead of taking root. When you stop treating your emotions as enemies, you begin living in relationship with them. The feelings you avoid don't disappear. They wait. And grow. Until hiding costs more than feeling.

Why We Learn to Run

When difficult emotions arise, most people learned early in life whether feelings were safe to express or dangerous to reveal. Developmental psychology shows that children absorb emotional regulation patterns from their caregivers during critical growth windows.[5] If parents respond to tears with comfort, children learn that sadness is manageable and connection is available during pain. If they respond with dismissal, frustration, or their own overwhelm, children can determine that expressing difficult emotions threatens their most important relationships. This creates what researchers refer to as "affect phobia," or the fear of your own feelings. If this sounds like you, your nervous system likely developed a window of tolerance, the range of emotional intensity you can experience while still feeling safe and functional. When emotions threatened to push you outside of this window as a child, particularly if adults couldn't help you regulate, your brain developed sophisticated avoidance strategies. These weren't conscious choices. They were adaptations that helped you survive environments where your feelings weren't safe.

The problem emerges when your childhood survival strategies become your adult operating systems. What protected you at eight limits you at thirty-eight. Steven Hayes, a clinical psychologist, describes this as experiential avoidance, the attempt to avoid or control internal experiences like thoughts, feelings, and sensations, even when doing so creates long-term harm.[6] Your brain develops increasingly elaborate strategies to keep you from feeling what you're afraid to feel. Staying constantly busy, using substances, compulsive behaviors, perfectionism, or any activity that keeps your attention directed away from your internal experience. Avoidance succeeds just long enough to trap you. The drink does numb the pain.

The work distracts from the loneliness. This intermittent reinforcement keeps you locked in the pattern because you never stay still long enough to discover that the feeling, when actually allowed, has a beginning, middle, and end.

Turning Toward What Hurts

Feeling, real feeling, begins with the radical act of pausing. Of creating space between you and your usual avoidance strategies long enough to notice what's actually happening in your body and your heart. Emotions, when allowed to move through you without resistance or avoidance, have a natural lifespan of about ninety seconds according to neuroanatomist Jill Bolte Taylor.[7] The wave rises, peaks, and falls if you don't fight it, analyze it, or try to make it go away. Most emotional suffering comes not from the feeling itself but from your resistance to feeling it. Staying present with difficult emotions requires what psychologist and researcher Kristin Neff calls self-compassion, the ability to hold your pain with the same tenderness you'd offer a suffering friend.[8] This isn't self-indulgence or wallowing. It's the recognition that your grief, fear, or loneliness deserves to be witnessed and cared for, not punished through avoidance.

Rebecca's transformation began in that gas station parking lot. Instead of immediately reaching for her usual escape routes, she let herself cry until the crying naturally stopped. She noticed the physical sensations without trying to make them go away. For the first time in three months, she said Cooper's name out loud. Told him she missed him. Let herself remember not just his death but his life. Something unexpected happened. The grief didn't destroy her. It hurt, oh boy did it hurt, but it also released something that had been building pressure for months. After twenty minutes of crying, Rebecca felt lighter than she had since the day Cooper died. Not happy, but honest. Not healed, but finally healing. Your feelings can't hurt you. Only your avoidance of them can. When you stop running, you discover that most feelings, when actually felt, are survivable. More than survivable. They often tell you what you need and show you why it matters.

When Both Options Serve The Moment

Distinguishing between necessary pauses and permanent escape determines whether you're practicing self-care or self-abandonment. Not every difficult moment requires you to drop everything and process immediately. Sometimes the most compassionate choice is to create intentional space between the trigger and the feeling. When you're presenting to a group and grief surges, compartmentalizing until you're alone is adaptive, not avoidant. When you're parenting a child through your own heartbreak, giving yourself permission to be functional at bedtime and to fall apart afterward allows you to meet both your needs and theirs. When trauma surfaces during a workday, acknowledging it and then scheduling time that evening to process it honors both your feelings and your responsibilities. This isn't running. It's choosing when and where you'll land.

The difference lives in your intention and timeline. Healthy distraction has specific endpoints and conscious plans for return. *I'm going to focus on work today and process my grief this evening. I'm going to watch this show to give my nervous system a rest, then I'll return to the difficult conversation.* These aren't vague somedays. They're concrete commitments to feel what needs feeling at a time when you have the capacity to hold it. Avoidance has no timeline because it has no intention of ever feeling what it's running from. It's an endless series of distractions designed to keep you perpetually numb, hoping that if you stay busy long enough the feelings will somehow disappear on their own. The meta-skill isn't just acknowledging what you feel, it's recognizing that the moment you stop running from your emotions, they stop chasing you.

Where This Choice Shows Up Every Day

Grief and Loss. When someone you love dies or a dream collapses, the instinct is often to stay in motion. Avoid fills every moment with activity, clearing out belongings before you feel ready and keeping you busy so stillness cannot catch up. Feel makes room for grief to arrive in its own timing. It gives you space to cry, remember, ache, and trust that the wave will soften without being pushed away.

Professional Pressure. Work intensifies, deadlines converge, and your body often knows something is wrong before your schedule reflects it. Avoid reacts by speeding up, adding more to your plate, and treating busyness like protection from stress. Feel slows the moment enough for you to notice what is happening inside. It helps you sort the truly urgent from the simply loud, so you respond with clarity instead of momentum.

Relationship Disconnection. Loneliness can settle quietly into the background of your days. Avoid fills the empty spaces with plans, screens, noise, and anything that keeps you from acknowledging the reality underneath. Feel lingers long enough to hear what the discomfort is signaling. It uncovers needs that have gone unmet, conversations that have been waiting, or connections that require repair rather than distraction.

Existential Anxiety. Questions about meaning and purpose often hover at the edges of daily life. Avoid pushes those questions aside with entertainment, substances, or relentless activity so there is no room for reflection to surface.

Feel turns toward the unease without demanding an immediate solution. It listens for what those questions are trying to show you about the life you want and the values that matter most.

Daily Discomfort. Some feelings arrive quietly. A hint of boredom. A restless ache. A soft sadness that drifts through the afternoon. Avoid reaches for the quick escape before you even register what you are experiencing, grabbing the phone or the snack or the distraction that keeps the moment at a distance. Feel pauses just long enough to name the sensation, understand what it is pointing toward, and allow it to move through instead of becoming another cycle of escape.

Practice Exercises: The Feeling Laboratory

These practices aren't about forcing yourself to feel everything all at once. They're about building tolerance for discomfort in small, survivable doses. Start with what feels manageable. The goal isn't to become someone who never avoids. It's to recognize when you're running and choose, sometimes, to stay.

The Ninety Second Experiment. When a difficult feeling arrives, set a timer for ninety seconds and stay with it. Notice the sensation without trying to fix it or find meaning in it. Feel where it settles in your body and breathe into that place instead of retreating from it. Watch the sensation rise, peak, and soften. Most feelings, when allowed to complete their natural rhythm, move through you more quickly than fear predicts. The body knows the cycle even when the mind insists the feeling will overwhelm. This practice shows you that discomfort can be survived and will eventually pass.

The Avoidance Audit. For one week, pay attention to the exact moment you reach for distraction. Catch the split second before you scroll, snack, pour a drink, or turn on the television.

Name what you were feeling just before you reached for something else. Over time, patterns become visible. The person who scrolls when lonely has different work than the one who takes on extra projects when feeling inadequate. Awareness creates interruption. Once you see how avoidance functions, you can gently choose to feel before the pattern takes over.

The Sensation Mapping Practice. When emotion feels overwhelming and your mind wants to escape into analysis, return to the body. Place your hand on the area where the feeling is strongest. Describe the sensation without judgment. Notice whether it is warm or cool, tight or open, moving or still. This simple shift interrupts mental spirals and anchors you in what is actually happening. The body often reveals where resistance lives and how you can stay present a little longer.

The Permission Practice. Each time you sense the urge to numb or distract, pause and give yourself permission to feel. Say the words aloud if you can. *I am allowed to feel anxious. I am allowed to feel sad. I am allowed to feel overwhelmed.* Naming the feeling softens your resistance and reminds your system that emotion is not a threat. It is an experience that can be held without falling apart.

The Present Moment Anchor. When avoidance begins to pull you away, ground yourself in the moment in front of you. Name a few things you can see. Notice the sounds in the room. Touch something near you and feel its texture. Then return to the question what is true right now. Often, you discover that this exact moment is manageable. Presence reduces urgency, steadies the nervous system, and builds trust that you can feel what arises without being consumed by it.

What Stillness Reveals

Rebecca learned to value stillness slowly in the months after her parking lot breakdown. She created room to grieve Cooper instead of outrunning the ache. She looked at photos without flinching. She cried when tears came. She talked about him without rushing past the tenderness. She noticed when she reached for distraction and asked herself what she was trying to avoid. Her days were still full, but the fullness now came from engagement rather than escape. She could sit in silence without panic. She could feel sadness without spiraling. She could rest without her mind scrambling to fill the space. Six months later, she adopted a new dog, not to replace Cooper but because she was ready to love again. Ready to risk loss because she knew she could survive grief. Ready to feel fully because avoiding had only kept her from living.

Each time you choose to feel rather than avoid, you reclaim a piece of your life from the exhausting work of running. It determines whether feelings overwhelm you or move through you. Whether your energy goes into numbing pain or tending to it. Whether your life keeps shrinking around what you fear or opens toward what matters. People who flee difficult emotions often describe never feeling at ease, never fully present, and never able to bring their whole selves into relationships. Joy stays muted because the full spectrum of feeling has been dulled. And the exhaustion becomes relentless because running leaves no place to rest.

When you stop running, your life no longer collapses around what you fear. You begin to inhabit yourself instead of managing yourself. Relationships shift because you are no longer offering only the parts that feel easiest to carry. Joy becomes steadier when you are not numbing the moments that precede it. A quieter kind of calm takes root when you stop battling your internal world. The feelings you avoided reveal themselves as survivable, often meaningful, sometimes even necessary. They show you what hurts, what matters, and what needs care. Your system knows how to move through emotion when you allow it the space to function. Strength was never the absence of emotion. It was the willingness to stay present as your experience unfolds. You can hold far more of your inner world than avoidance ever allowed you to believe.

3

Blame or Build

the grievance that consumes you

Ethan had been documenting his neighbor's violations for six months, and tonight he was finally going to post the evidence that would vindicate him. The cursor blinked in the NextDoor text field at 11:34 p.m. while his heart hammered with the righteousness and rage that had become his default state. The Excel spreadsheet on his second monitor glowed like a shrine to his grievance. Date and timestamp in column A. Violation type in column B. Photographic evidence notes in column C. Six months of data, color-coded by severity, cross-referenced with HOA bylaws and city ordinances. The guy at 2847 had no idea what was coming.

Ethan's kitchen table had become a war room. Printed screenshots fanned across every surface. His phone sat within constant reach, notifications enabled for every NextDoor post, every comment on the ongoing saga that had turned his quiet suburban street into the neighborhood's most-watched reality show. The trash bin violations alone filled seventeen rows. Music audible after 10 p.m. appeared fourteen times with decibel readings. Packages blocking the shared walkway documented twenty-three obstructions. The car parked across both driveways had nine separate incidents, each photographed from multiple angles. Tonight's post would be different. Tonight, he had video evidence, a petition signed by three other homeowners, and expert analysis of property value impact from someone who claimed to be a realtor. He'd spent four hours crafting the message. Professional but firm. Detailed but not petty. Righteous but not aggressive. It was perfect.

His phone buzzed with a text from his sister asking if he was coming to Mom's birthday dinner Sunday. She hadn't heard from him in weeks. Ethan set the phone face down without finishing the message. Family stuff could wait. This was important. Another buzz, this time from NextDoor. Someone named ConcernedResident2824 had posted something new. Ethan's stomach tightened even before he clicked. "Anyone else notice Ethan from 2845 has made 49 posts about trash cans in the last six months? Maybe time to get a hobby?" The post already had seventeen likes and eight comments. "Seriously, dude needs to touch grass. I've started skipping his posts. The irony of someone this obsessed with rules becoming the neighborhood problem." They were turning this around on him. Making him the villain when he was the one trying to maintain property values, trying to keep the community livable, trying to hold people accountable! Ethan's hands started shaking as he opened a new draft post, fingers flying with furious energy. "To everyone making jokes at my expense, maybe if more people held their neighbors accountable instead of letting everything slide…"

He stopped mid-sentence. The cursor blinked, waiting. On the counter behind his laptop sat an unopened letter from his employer's HR department about his performance review being delayed pending discussion of workplace concerns. Next to it, three unread books about the career change he'd been planning for two years. A postcard from his best friend's wedding in Cabo that he'd skipped because he couldn't leave town during the violations. For six months, Ethan had averaged ninety minutes per day on this. Documenting. Posting. Arguing in comment sections. Refreshing for responses. That was 270 hours. An entire work month invested in proving someone else was wrong while his actual life quietly dismantled itself. His neighbor was living his life, mostly unaware that Ethan existed, while Ethan had organized his entire existence around grievances he was collecting, validation he was seeking, and vindication that never quite arrived. His cursor still blinked in that text field. One click and he could post his response, spend another evening defending his position, feeling that surge of righteous anger. Or he could face what those 270 hours had cost him and ask a question that terrified him: What could he have built with all this energy he'd spent on blame?

Why Your Choice Matters

The mental ledger you keep of other people's failures is written in your own time. Each entry costs you hours you'll never recover, energy you could have invested elsewhere, attention that might have built something worth having. That running commentary explaining why things aren't working feels like a clear-eyed assessment of reality. *Bad things always happen to me. Other people get away with everything. Nobody respects the rules.* It feels like justice, like refusing to be a passive victim of other people's thoughtlessness. But that clarity is actually a trap disguised as wisdom. Your evidence of their guilt becomes nothing more than proof of your own paralysis.

Martin Seligman, a psychologist and founder of positive psychology, first described learned helplessness as a state in which repeated experiences of feeling powerless lead people to stop trying to change their circumstances, even when change is possible. In his later work with explanatory style, he showed that helplessness in humans is shaped by how wc habitually explain what goes wrong in our lives.[9] When your default is a pessimistic style, you come to see negative events as permanent, pervasive, and outside your control, and this pattern powerfully increases the risk of helplessness and depression. Every offense confirms that people are failing you. Every disappointment proves that life is unfair. Every limitation becomes evidence that change is impossible until others change first. You're not discovering truth. You're spending your time proving a point that changes nothing.

This creates what psychologists call external locus of control, the belief that your life is primarily shaped by factors outside your influence. When you're unhappy, it's because of what they did. When you're stuck, it's because they won't do what you want. When you're suffering, it's because they refuse to be reasonable. The narrative feels accurate because you can point to real violations, actual thoughtlessness, and genuine unfairness. But *accurate* and *useful* are not the same thing. Blame might correctly identify who's wrong, but it can never tell you what to build with your one finite life. Even worse, being right about their failure doesn't make you less stuck in yours.

Build operates from a different premise entirely. You always have a choice about where you invest your attention, energy, and time. These investments compound into your actual lived experience, while other people's behavior remains largely irrelevant to what you create. When you choose build over blame, you stop needing others to change before you can move forward. You stop asking why they won't change and start paying attention to what's actually yours. This transformation isn't about denying that others sometimes behave badly or pretending that legitimate grievances don't exist. It's about recognizing a simple mathematical truth. The hours you spend cataloging failures are hours you don't spend creating success. Your grievances cost you your growth.

Why We Invest in Being Right

The blaming narrative offers something seductive. It lets you feel superior while remaining stuck. When your neighbor is inconsiderate, you get to be the considerate one. When others break rules, you get to be principled. When people behave badly, you get to be right. This moral high ground feels like power, but it's actually a sophisticated form of powerlessness. You've made your emotional state dependent on other people's behavior. Your peace contingent on their choices. Your well-being tethered to their consideration. The righteousness feels validating, but the validation comes at the cost of your agency. This pattern took root when you were genuinely powerless. As a child facing unfair treatment from adults or cruelty from peers, blaming them protected your sense of self-worth. You couldn't control their behavior, but you could control the meaning you made of it. The story that they were wrong and you were right kept you from internalizing their behavior as evidence of your inadequacy.

This worked beautifully during childhood. A 7-year-old can't make parents stop fighting, can't make teachers stop playing favorites, can't make bullies stop bullying. The narrative that it's not about me, it's about them was adaptive, protective, and necessary for psychological survival. But the same story that once protected you now confines you. You're no longer powerless in most situations. You have choices about where you live, who you spend time with, what you invest energy in, and how you respond to provocations. Yet your brain keeps running the childhood program. Collect evidence of wrongdoing, build the case for your righteousness, wait for vindication that will prove you were right all along. The pattern persists not because it serves you now, but because it's wired so deeply from when it did serve you.

Albert Bandura, a psychologist and pioneer of social cognitive theory, introduced the concept of self-efficacy to describe how your belief in your own capabilities shapes what you attempt, how long you persist, and how you interpret setbacks.[10] When you focus on what others are doing wrong, you stop focusing on what you could build instead. When you stop building, you don't create new possibilities. When you don't create new possibilities, you accumulate evidence that nothing you do matters. Only what they do matters. The digital age amplifies this trap exponentially. Social media gives you an audience for your grievances. Every post about what's wrong gets likes from people who share your outrage. Your blaming narrative receives social rewards that make it even harder to shift your attention toward building. The dopamine hit from validation feels like progress, but it's actually reinforcing the pattern that keeps you stuck.

Redirecting Your Energy

Build emerges the moment you recognize a simple truth about time. Every minute spent documenting what's wrong with others is a minute you're not spending creating what's right with your own life. This realization hit Ethan three weeks after the NextDoor incident, when he caught himself mid-scroll through neighborhood violations and asked a question he'd been avoiding. *What am I actually building here?* The answer was devastating in its clarity. Nothing. He was maintaining a case nobody cared about while his actual life, the career change he wanted, the relationships that mattered, the health he'd neglected, waited for energy he kept spending on blame. He closed the app. Not because his neighbor suddenly became considerate, but because being right about someone else's failures would never compensate for his own unrealized potential.

Gabriele Oettingen, a psychologist who developed the concept of mental contrasting and the Wish-Outcome-Obstacle-Plan (WOOP) method, has shown that real change requires holding both a vivid picture of your desired future and a clear view of your current obstacles at the same time, then forming specific plans to close the gap.[11] Fantasizing about a better life without acknowledging barriers tends to lower effort and follow-through, while dwelling on obstacles without envisioning what you want leaves you stuck in place. Mental contrasting interrupts both patterns, transforming stuck energy into momentum by helping you see what you want, identify the barriers that truly stand in your way, and commit to your specific next step. Ethan redirected that same analytical energy he'd used to document violations toward building his career transition. He filed one formal complaint with the HOA, then deleted NextDoor and invested those reclaimed ninety minutes daily into professional certifications.

Within three months, Ethan had completed two certifications he'd been too busy to pursue. Within six months, he'd landed the new role he'd been planning for years. His mornings shifted from checking violations to building skills. His evenings moved from crafting righteous posts to having dinner with friends. The violations still happened. Trash bins still appeared late. Music still played after 10 p.m. But these facts consumed zero seconds of Ethan's day because he was too busy building his own life to notice. The problem didn't disappear. It became irrelevant. You don't need others to change. You need to stop giving them power over what you create.

When Both Serve Options the Moment

Sometimes acknowledging that someone else's behavior is genuinely problematic serves you. When facing harassment, discrimination, abuse, or violations of legitimate agreements, naming the problem and seeking appropriate redress is essential. Setting clear boundaries, filing formal complaints, or ending relationships with people who repeatedly violate reasonable standards isn't blame. It's self-protection. Some situations genuinely require collective action, formal complaints, or systemic change rather than individual accommodation. Legal violations, safety concerns, and contractual breaches deserve formal response through appropriate channels. The distinction matters because not every acknowledgment of wrong is blame, and not every response to harm is righteousness. The key question is whether your response actually builds a solution.

Useful acknowledgment says this behavior is unacceptable, here's what I'm doing about it, and then I'm moving forward with building my life. Useless blame says this behavior is unacceptable, and I will continue documenting it indefinitely while my life revolves around proving how wrong they are. One is a step toward resolution and redirection. The other is an identity built around being wronged. Build consciousness doesn't mean accepting genuine harm. It means responding to harm strategically and then redirecting your energy toward creating what you want. You can address real problems while refusing to let those problems consume your life. Blame serves accurate assessment when it helps you recognize genuine problems and take effective action. Build serves empowerment when it helps you invest your energy in creating what you want rather than documenting what you don't want. The meta-skill isn't just choosing to build instead of blame, it's recognizing that your finite energy is always in motion, and only one direction compounds.

Where This Choice Shows Up Every Day

Neighborhood Dynamics. Hours spent tracking noise, violations, and online arguments leave you tense and hyper-focused on what others are doing wrong. Blame turns your home into a surveillance post. Build shifts your attention toward creating a space you enjoy, improving what you can touch, and nurturing the neighbor relationships that feel healthy. Your home becomes a place you shape rather than a place you defend.

Workplace Situations. Keeping score of colleagues' mistakes drains energy you could use for your own growth. Blame circles the same frustrations without movement. Build redirects that attention into developing your skills, strengthening your network, and preparing for the roles you want. Your progress stops depending on anyone else's performance.

Family Patterns. Replaying old hurts and measuring every slight keeps you anchored to past versions of your family. Blame catalogues injury with precision. Build shifts your focus toward the relationships you want to strengthen or the boundaries that give you peace. You create the closeness or stability you once waited for others to provide.

Online Spaces. Arguing with strangers and refreshing notifications turns your digital life into a grievance loop. Blame rewards outrage with more outrage. Build uses that same time to learn, make, or engage with communities that nourish you. Your online presence begins to reflect what you value instead of what irritates you.

Relationship Dynamics. Focusing on your partner's shortcomings narrows the entire relationship to a list of unmet expectations. Blame waits for them to finally change. Build invests in connection through your own choices, steady conversations, and clarity about what you can and cannot live with. The relationship shifts because you take responsibility for what is actually yours.

Practice Exercises: The Redirect

Redirecting blame doesn't mean pretending harm never happened. These practices invite you to track where your attention goes, reclaim the energy you've been spending on what others should do, and quietly return it to what you're actually able to shape.

Energy Audit. Spend one week noticing where your mental and emotional effort goes. Pay attention to how often your thoughts drift toward someone else's mistakes and how little time is left for what you want to create. Write down the moments when blame takes over. Estimate the hours it occupies. Then ask what those hours could support if you redirected them. This practice makes the cost of blame visible and shows you where choice returns.

The "So What?" Test. When blame surfaces, pause and ask what you plan to do next. If the answer is to keep tracking the problem or wait for someone else to change, you're still choosing blame. If the answer involves something you can influence, move there. This question turns complaint into movement by revealing whether you are solving something or sustaining it.

Circle Mapping. Write down the situation that's upsetting you. Create two simple columns. One side holds what you can shape through your own choices. The other holds what lies outside your control. Invest your effort only in the part that belongs to you. Give the second column one necessary action if needed, then release it. This exercise clarifies where your power actually lives and protects you from trying to build in places you cannot reach.

The Build Question. Before posting a complaint, sending a reactive message, or replaying someone's shortcomings, ask whether this action moves you toward what you want or simply rehearses what you dislike. If it's the latter, pause and redirect your attention toward something more constructive. This interrupts the blame reflex in the exact moment you regain agency.

Language Shift. Notice the tone of your internal dialogue. Blame speaks in absolutes and grievances. Shift the language toward what supports growth, even in small ways. Let your thoughts point toward what you'd rather create than what you resent. Watch how this gentle change in tone alters what feels possible as your focus moves from frustration toward forward motion.

The Mathematics of Momentum

Six months after Ethan chose build, he had a new career, restored family relationships, completed a half-marathon, and started the business he had been too busy to attempt. His neighbor still left trash bins out late. But that fact no longer consumed Ethan's attention. Not because the neighbor changed, but because Ethan finally stopped giving the situation any space in his life. The problem did not disappear. It simply stopped determining the shape of his days.

Each time you choose build over blame, your time shifts back into your own hands. What once went toward documenting what is wrong begins to support what you want to create. This is not abstract transformation. It's simple math. The difference between spending 270 hours tracking a neighbor's habits and spending 270 hours developing your own potential. Between maintaining spreadsheets of others' failures and shaping a career that reflects who you are becoming.

The arithmetic is stark. Those hours either expand your life or evaporate into complaints that change nothing.

The cost of chronic blame shows up everywhere. In your bank account, your resume, your relationships, your body. While you were cataloging someone else's inconsideration, you missed the development that would have carried you forward. While you were arguing with strangers online, you skipped the gym, ignored your partner, forgot to call your mother. The ledger is honest. Time spent blaming is time not spent building, and what you invest in blame is gone forever. Building works differently. Each hour you invest creates something that steadies or strengthens the next thing. The certification leads to the interview. The interview leads to the job. The job leads to the network. The network leads to opportunities you could not have imagined when your attention was tied to monitoring someone else's choices. Build creates momentum. Blame creates quicksand. One keeps you moving. The other pulls you back into the same frustrations without relief.

That is what becomes possible when you reclaim the time and effort that blame once consumed. You do not need others to change. You need to stop handing them the authority to direct your life. The person who chooses build discovers something steadying. You cannot control what others do, but you can decide what you create with the resources you have. What you nurture grows. What you rehearse repeats. Choosing build over blame becomes the quiet foundation for everything that follows. The question is not whether others behave differently. The question is what you want the next six months of your life to become.

4

Chase or Content

the treadmill that goes nowhere

Sierra stood on the deck of a chartered yacht in the Galapagos Islands watching a blue-footed booby perform its mating dance three feet away, and all she could think about was whether Patagonia was better. She'd saved for this trip for six months. Worked doubles on weekends. Said no to her best friend's bachelorette party. Ate meal-prepped chicken and rice while her roommates ordered takeout. She was 27 years old, standing in front of one of the planet's most extraordinary creatures, and her thumb was scrolling Instagram trying to figure out if she'd made the wrong choice.

Her friend Hannah had just posted from Torres del Paine, granite peaks rising behind her in light that looked better than anything Sierra had photographed here. The caption read "Sometimes you just know you're exactly where you're supposed to be" with a prayer hands emoji. One thousand forty-three likes in eleven minutes. Sierra's blue-footed booby post from this morning had gotten only 807 likes in two hours. Hannah's Patagonia glacier photo from yesterday got over 10,000. Sierra felt the familiar tightening in her stomach that had followed her across twenty-eight countries. The sense that she was somehow always in the wrong place, seeing the less-impressive version, choosing the location that would photograph well, but not well enough.

The yacht's naturalist guide was explaining the booby's hunting patterns. Sierra's fingers opened a new browser tab searching for flights to Patagonia, Chile. Twelve hundred dollars from Quito. She'd done this exact thing in Iceland while planning this trip. Did it in Japan while planning Morocco. Did it in Morocco while planning New Zealand. Twenty-eight countries, and she'd stood in each one calculating the next, measuring whether what she was experiencing was impressive enough to justify not already being somewhere else. Her restaurant shifts funded the flights. Her travel content funded the accommodations. The system worked until she looked up from her phone long enough to realize she couldn't remember most of what she'd actually seen.

She kept a map on her apartment wall with pins marking every place she'd been, but when she looked at it, she mostly saw the gaps. The blank spaces that made her wall look emptier than if she'd never started traveling at all. Each pin represented a place that had felt urgent to reach and ordinary within days of arrival. Each destination had promised to be the one that finally satisfied. And each one had delivered a few days of contentment before revealing another gap, another place that suddenly seemed more impressive. The satisfaction she'd imagined kept moving the moment she arrived. She had eighteen unfinished travel journals and 40,000 photos she'd never looked at after posting.

Her phone buzzed. Her mother's text showed a kitchen with new white subway tile and brass fixtures, the same kitchen Sierra had eaten breakfast in for eighteen years, now renovated for the third time since college. "Finally got the kitchen I always wanted!" Sierra's jaw clenched. Her mother had spent thirty years upgrading that house. New furniture when the current set was perfectly good. All that stuff, all that accumulation, that treadmill of wanting the next version of what she already had. Sierra had sworn she'd live differently. No mortgage. No possessions weighing her down. Just experiences, just freedom. But standing on this boat with a browser tab open to Patagonia flights, something landed that made her hands shake. Her mother's third kitchen. She was already planning her twenty-ninth country before she'd finished the twenty-eighth. Same treadmill. Different currency. Never satisfied.

The guide announced an early departure for Darwin Bay tomorrow. Sierra's mind spun ahead. Maybe she could skip tomorrow, fly back early, and save the expenses for Patagonia. Or she could stay, actually be here, let the trip she'd saved six months for be enough. The choice wasn't about Darwin Bay or Patagonia. It was about whether she'd keep running on a treadmill that moved faster the harder she chased it, or whether she'd finally stop long enough to ask if satisfaction was something she'd ever find at the next destination, or if it had been waiting here all along.

Why Your Choice Matters

You've been chasing your whole life and calling it living. The next thing that will finally make you feel complete. The accomplishment that will prove you've made it. The acquisition that will fill whatever's been missing. Each thing you chase promises to be the last thing you'll need to chase, the one that will let you finally stop and feel satisfied. But satisfaction keeps moving. You reach the summit and immediately see the next peak. You achieve the goal, and within weeks, the goalpost shifts. You get what you wanted and want something else before you've even absorbed having it. The currency changes across generations, but the mechanism stays the same. One generation chased the house in the suburbs and the new car in the driveway. Another chased the bigger house in the better neighborhood and the boat in the marina. Another chased the passport stamps and the restaurant experiences and the festivals. The next will chase whatever becomes the new signal that you've arrived. Whether you're collecting possessions or experiences, the pattern persists.

Each thing stops mattering shortly after you get it. Your brain adapts. The thrill fades. What felt like finally arriving becomes just another thing you once wanted and now barely notice. Psychologist Dan Gilbert, a leading researcher on affective forecasting, has shown that this happens because we consistently overestimate how much happiness future achievements will bring and drastically underestimate how quickly we'll adapt to them once they arrive.[12] That house you thought would change everything? You adapted within months. That promotion you sacrificed years for? The satisfaction lasted far less time than you imagined. That dream trip you saved for? You were planning the next one before you'd even finished this one. Contentment isn't waiting to be acquired. It's waiting to be practiced.

Your brain's hedonic adaptation ensures whatever you get stops mattering quickly. Social comparison means you're always measuring yourself against people who have more, different, or better. Scroll for five minutes and you'll find ten people collecting what you're still chasing. These forces interlock into a system that guarantees exhaustion. You achieve something, adapt to it, compare yourself to others, feel behind, then chase the next thing. The cycle never breaks because you're treating satisfaction like something you haven't found yet instead of something you haven't learned yet. Sierra thought she'd escaped the treadmill by choosing experiences over possessions, but the mechanism doesn't care what currency you're chasing.

The twenty-eighth country felt exactly like her mother's latest kitchen remodel. Momentarily exciting and then immediately ordinary. She kept running because she'd never learned to stop.

Why We Never Feel Satisfied

Your need to keep chasing didn't start with Instagram or travel culture. It started with a brain designed for survival in a world where enough never existed. When our ancestors faced genuine scarcity, the humans who survived were the ones who never stopped seeking more. More food. More resources. More security. The brain that felt satisfied stopped preparing. The brain that kept wanting kept surviving. You inherited that drive. The problem is that the scarcity that shaped this system no longer matches the world you're living in.

Psychologist and happiness researcher Sonja Lyubomirsky has shown that our minds rapidly adapt to changes in circumstances, a process known as hedonic adaptation.[13] This helps explain why lasting gains in happiness don't automatically follow from external success. Your brain recalibrates its baseline after every positive change, returning you to roughly the same level of happiness regardless of what you achieve or acquire. Win the lottery, get the dream job, travel to your bucket list destination, and within months you're back where you started emotionally. But you don't recognize this as biological recalibration. You interpret it as evidence you haven't found the right thing yet.

Modern culture doesn't just enable this pattern. It systematically exploits it. Advertising manufactures desire for things you didn't know you wanted. Social media algorithms curate feeds that maximize engagement by showing you people slightly ahead of where you are, the perfect distance to trigger inadequacy without creating hopelessness. Every platform is engineered to make you feel like you're missing something. Social psychologist Leon Festinger, who first proposed social comparison theory to explain how we evaluate ourselves by comparing to others, did his work in small, face-to-face groups in the 1950s.[14] He could not have imagined a world where your comparison group would be effectively infinite and curated specifically to make you feel insufficient. The comparison that once helped you assess your standing in a small tribe now happens constantly against thousands of people whose curated lives make your actual life look inadequate.

The currency your culture values becomes the metric you use to measure whether you're enough. But the measurement system is designed to keep you wanting. The goalpost moves every time you get close. What felt impressive last year becomes the baseline this year. What your peers are collecting becomes your new measure. You're not chasing things because they'll make you happy. You're chasing them because not having them makes you feel behind in a race with no finish line. So you keep searching, acquiring, experiencing, convinced the next achievement will be different. The adaptation mechanism that once kept you motivated to survive now keeps you perpetually dissatisfied with what should be more than enough.

Learning to Stop the Chase

Three days after standing on that yacht calculating Patagonia costs, Sierra made a choice that terrified her. She told Hannah she wasn't going to chase Patagonia next. She was going to stay home for six months. The decision felt like giving up, like admitting defeat, like watching everyone else collect experiences while she stood still. But the truth was simpler and harder. She'd been running for five years and couldn't remember where she'd been. Each destination had promised to finally satisfy and each one had left her planning the next before she'd even unpacked. The problem wasn't that she needed better destinations. The problem was that she'd been treating satisfaction like something waiting at the next pin on her map instead of something she could practice right here.

The shift started small. She stopped scrolling travel content first thing in the morning. When the urge hit to research flights, she noticed it without obeying it. She started asking herself what she was afraid would happen if she didn't chase the next thing. The answer came quickly. That she'd become boring. That she'd have nothing to show for her life. That staying still meant settling. But when she actually looked at her life without comparing it to everyone else's, she realized she no longer knew what she wanted. She only knew what looked impressive. She'd been chasing other people's definitions of enough and calling it her own ambition.

She started practicing contentment with what she already had. Cooking dinner without photographing it. Taking walks without tracking them. Sitting in her apartment on Saturday night without needing somewhere better to be. The practice felt uncomfortable at first, like her brain kept reaching for the next thing to want. But slowly, something shifted. She noticed her neighborhood had a bakery she'd walked past a hundred times without seeing. She started conversations with the woman at the farmers market. She remembered what it felt like to want something for herself instead of wanting it because it would look good to other people. Satisfaction wasn't waiting at the next destination. It was available right here in the practice of letting what she had be enough.

When Both Options Serve the Moment

Ambition isn't the same as restless pursuit, and contentment isn't the same as settling. Sometimes growth requires reaching for something beyond your current capacity, stretching toward goals that demand your development, pursuing opportunities that will expand who you are. The distinction lives in whether you're moving toward something meaningful or running away from feeling inadequate without it. Healthy ambition has a purpose beyond motion itself. It builds something, serves something, and develops something real. Restless chasing just keeps you busy enough to avoid stillness, where discomfort might surface. Your parents weren't wrong for wanting the bigger house if it genuinely served their family's needs, and you're not shallow for wanting travel experiences if they genuinely feed your curiosity about the world.

The question isn't whether to have goals or desire new experiences. It's whether those goals emerge from genuine values or from comparison-driven inadequacy. Do you want this thing because it aligns with who you're becoming, or because someone else having it makes you feel less-than without it? Are you pursuing this experience because it genuinely interests you, or because documenting it will prove something to people who are barely paying attention? Sierra's mother bought the bigger house because her neighbors did. Sierra booked exotic trips because her feed suggested she should. The mechanism is identical even when the currency changes. Chase stops serving you the moment it becomes about proving worth rather than expressing it.

Content becomes possible when you stop measuring your life against everyone else's and start asking what would actually satisfy you if no one was watching. Sierra learned this when she planned her first trip after the six-month pause. She chose a place that genuinely interested her rather than one that would photograph well. She stayed long enough to feel something rather than just document it. She stopped posting for validation and started traveling for her own curiosity. Her wanting came from internal curiosity rather than external comparison. The meta-skill isn't just about managing your acquisitions or moderating your ambitions. It's about distinguishing desire that expands you from desire that only keeps you running.

Where This Choice Shows Up Every Day

Professional Life. Your colleague gets promoted and suddenly your own role feels inadequate. Chase researches the next position, updates your resume, angles for visibility, treats your current work as a stepping stone instead of a contribution. Content focuses on mastery in the role you have, finds satisfaction in work done well, and pursues growth when it serves genuine development rather than the pressure to prove you are moving fast enough.

Intimate Relationships. Your partner mentions a friend's engagement and pressure rises around your own timeline. Chase starts planning the proposal, researching rings, rushing toward milestones because it feels like everyone else is already there. Content stays present with the relationship you are actually building, lets depth grow at its own pace, and chooses commitment when it emerges from readiness rather than comparison.

Family Dynamics. Your sibling buys a house and your rental suddenly feels temporary and insufficient. Chase scrolls real estate apps, calculates mortgages you cannot afford, and treats your current space as something to escape. Content makes your home feel like home, invests in the life you are living now, and considers homeownership only when it serves your actual needs rather than proving you are keeping up.

Friendships. Friends post about a gathering you were not invited to and discomfort sets in. Chase fills your calendar, accepts every invitation, and treats social activity like evidence of belonging. Content deepens the relationships you already have, says no without anxiety, and measures connection by quality instead of quantity.

Daily Life. You walk through your apartment noticing everything that could be upgraded. Chase browses for new furniture, compares better versions of what you already own, and keeps the space feeling unfinished. Content uses and appreciates what is here, repairs what needs attention, and lets your home be the place where your actual life happens rather than a project that always needs improving.

Practice Exercises: The CHASE Audit

These practices help you watch, in real time, how your attention slides from enough into "not quite yet." They're about noticing when the hunt for upgrades has stopped adding joy and started eroding it, so you can gently step off the treadmill for a moment and feel what's already here.

C – Catch yourself mid-scroll. The moment you notice yourself researching the next thing, comparing what you have to what others have, or feeling that familiar pull toward more, stop. Whether you're browsing upgrades for your home, planning your next trip, scrolling beauty products, or checking who got promoted, name what you're doing. *I'm chasing again.* This simple recognition interrupts the automatic pattern before it gains momentum.

H – Hold it against the three-month test. Ask yourself how long the last three things you acquired continued to satisfy you. That purchase, experience, achievement, treatment, or upgrade. Be brutally honest. Did they still matter three months later, or were you already wanting the next version? This question reveals the pattern your brain doesn't want you to see. The treadmill keeps moving because you keep believing this time will be different.

A – Appreciate something you already have. Before chasing anything new, spend ten minutes fully engaging with something you already own, somewhere you already are, or someone you already know. Cook with what's in your kitchen. Wear the clothes already in your closet. Spend time with people you keep saying you'll see more of. Notice what's available when you're not measuring it against what you don't have yet. Contentment lives in attention, not acquisition.

S – Subtract the audience. Ask yourself if you'd still want this thing if no one would ever know you had it. Remove the feed, remove the validation, remove every external measure of whether this makes you impressive. What remains? If the answer is "not much," you're chasing for comparison, not genuine desire. If something real remains, that's worth exploring without the performance.

E – Experience enough for one day. Choose one 24-hour period where you don't research, plan, or pursue anything new. No scrolling for upgrades. No planning the next milestone. No browsing what you could buy, do, achieve, or become. Just be with what's already here. Notice how much energy you've been spending on the chase and how much satisfaction is available when you stop running long enough to feel where you already are.

When Enough Becomes Enough

Eight months after standing on that yacht in the Galapagos, Sierra sat in her neighborhood coffee shop on a Saturday morning with no plans and no urgency to create any. Her friend Hannah texted asking if she wanted to split an Airbnb in Portugal next month. Sierra's first instinct was the old familiar pull. *Yes. Book it now before it's gone.* But she paused. Noticed the wanting without obeying it. She asked herself the questions that had become practice. Would this genuinely interest her, or was she chasing because Hannah was going? Would she remember this trip in three months, or would it become another pin on a map she barely looked at? She texted back honestly. "I'm going to pass. Trying to actually be somewhere instead of always planning the next place." Hannah responded within seconds. "Honestly? Same. I'm exhausted."

Sierra still traveled, but her relationship to it had fundamentally shifted. She'd chosen one place last spring and stayed three weeks instead of hitting four countries in ten days. She left her phone in the apartment most afternoons. She came home with seven photos and memories she could actually recall without scrolling through her camera roll. The map on her wall looked different now. She'd stopped adding pins as proof of everywhere she'd been. The blank spaces that used to make her feel behind now felt like breathing room instead of inadequacy. She'd been so focused on filling gaps that she hadn't realized the chase was wearing her down.

Her mother texted photos of another kitchen upgrade last month. Sierra felt the old judgment rising, then caught it. Her mother was chasing contentment the same way Sierra had been, just with different currency. She called instead of texting. "The kitchen looks beautiful, Mom. Are you happy with it?" Her mother paused, then laughed softly. "You know what? I think I finally am." They both heard what the other wasn't saying. Sierra still felt the pull sometimes. Saw friends posting from places she hadn't been and felt that familiar tightness. But she'd learned to notice the wanting without obeying it. The satisfaction she'd been chasing across twenty-eight countries had been waiting here all along, not in the next destination but in the practice of letting this one be enough.

5

Control or Surrender

the grip that gives nothing back

Samantha stared at three notifications glowing on her phone at 6:47 a.m., each one a small failure in the elaborate apparatus she'd built to keep her father safe. Medication app alert: "Robert Harris missed evening dose - Lisinopril 10mg." Nest camera motion alert: "No activity detected in Robert Harris kitchen - 16 hours." Text from her father, sent at 10:17 p.m.: "Stop checking on me. I'm fine."

She'd installed the cameras six months ago after he forgot to turn off the stove. The medication app came four months later after he mixed up his pills. Then the shared calendar coordinating his appointments, the weekly grocery delivery she ordered, the daily check-in calls at exactly 8 a.m. Each mechanism designed to catch what had started slipping. Late at night, when sleep wouldn't come, Samantha updated the spreadsheet on her laptop. Color-coded cells tracking medication compliance, mobility incidents, and cognitive markers. She told herself this was responsible caregiving, that the knot in her stomach at 3 a.m. meant that she was doing what any responsible daughter would do.

Her father was 74. Still drove. Still gardened. Still played poker every Thursday with the same men he'd known for forty years. He lived in the house where Samantha had grown up, where her mother had died three years ago. But Samantha had been cataloging each small decline. The repeated questions. The bills with late fees. The morning she'd found him still in pajamas at noon. She kept a detailed spreadsheet because monitoring meant caring, because if she tracked enough data points she could prevent what terrified her most. Last week her sister Charlotte said something that kept echoing. "You're not helping him age with dignity. You're managing his decline like a project."

Now her phone was ringing. Meadowbrook Senior Living, the facility she'd been researching for eight months. "Ms. Harris, we have an unexpected opening in our independent living wing. We need to know by 5 p.m. today." Samantha's hands started shaking. Eight months of waitlist, now she had less than ten hours to decide. She knew the statistics by heart. Falls, medication errors, isolation. Meadowbrook had twenty-four hour oversight, medication coordination, emergency response. The responsible choice that would let her sleep instead of jerking awake at 3 a.m. She could already feel the relief spreading through her chest, the fantasy of sharing this responsibility with professionals trained for exactly this. But beneath that relief was a dread she didn't yet understand.

Her father didn't want to move. He'd told her repeatedly, each time more firmly. But he didn't see the risks clearly, didn't understand how quickly things could deteriorate. She had medical power of attorney, signed over when her mother was dying. She could present this logically, walk him through the numbers. Or show up with the brochure and her practiced arguments, the same approach that had worked with the medication app and the cameras. Wear him down with reason and concern until agreeing felt easier than resisting. But there was another possibility she kept trying to ignore. What if what was stealing her father's independence wasn't age or decline? What if it was her?

Twenty minutes later, Samantha stood in her father's garden holding the Meadowbrook brochure, watching him look at her with something she'd never seen before. Not gratitude. Not appreciation. Something that looked like defeat. "You've already decided, haven't you?" She started listing the benefits. The oversight. The protection. The peace of mind. When she finished, he said something that struck harder than she expected. "I survived seventy-four years without you controlling every breath I take." In the next few minutes, Samantha would either call Meadowbrook and secure the spot, or face something more terrifying than any missed medication: that her need to control his well-being was destroying the very thing she was trying to protect.

Why Your Choice Matters

The more you try to control, the more out of control you actually become. The mental exhaustion of trying to orchestrate everyone else's emotions. The physical strain of working endless hours to prevent any possible failure. Control feels like strength, like responsibility, like the only mature response when so much is at stake. You tell yourself that careful oversight prevents disaster, that monitoring equals protection, that if you just track enough data points you can guarantee the outcomes that matter most. But the paradox is devastating. The harder you grip, the more slips away.

Psychologist Ellen Langer, who first named the illusion of control, showed that people often behave as if they can influence outcomes that are in reality determined by chance.[15] Her experiments found that when situations contain "skill cues" like choice, competition, or involvement, people's confidence in their personal impact rises far beyond what the objective probabilities justify. They develop elaborate tracking systems and rituals around results they cannot actually affect and then interpret random successes as proof that their effort or vigilance made the difference. Samantha's color-coded spreadsheet tracking her father's cognitive decline wasn't keeping him safer. It was giving her the comforting illusion that documentation equaled prevention, that enough surveillance could somehow stop aging itself. This illusion serves a crucial psychological function. It protects you from the helplessness of caring deeply about outcomes you cannot control. But the protection can cost you everything worth protecting.

Control begins with a convincing promise. That effort equals influence. That monitoring equals security. That if you just work hard enough, track carefully enough, and intervene quickly enough, you can guarantee the results that matter most to you. Your father won't fall. Your children won't fail. Your partner won't disappoint you. Nothing important will slip out of your hands. But surrender reveals what control obscures. Your real power lies not in controlling what happens, but in choosing your response to whatever happens. Control is fear posing as love. When you choose surrender over control, you stop trying to prevent your father from aging, your children from struggling, or your partner from making mistakes. You start trusting that the people you love are more capable than your fear suggests. That life can unfold without your constant intervention. That protection and surveillance are not the same thing.

This isn't about passivity or abandoning people who depend on you. It's about distinguishing between what you can genuinely influence and what you're burning yourself out trying to orchestrate. Samantha discovered this when her father's eleven words cracked something open. She'd been so focused on preventing every possible medical crisis that she'd been creating a different kind of emergency. Her surveillance hadn't been keeping him secure. It had been keeping her from feeling the unbearable terror of watching someone she loved age beyond her ability to control it.

Why We Tighten Our Grip

The roots of control patterns often trace back to childhood experiences with unpredictable environments. Developmental psychologist Mary Ainsworth, who extended attachment theory through her research, showed how early caregiving patterns shape a child's strategies for staying close to safety.[16] Children who experience inconsistent care often develop what she called anxious (insecure-ambivalent) attachment, characterized by constant monitoring and attempts to control their surroundings. Her work showed that when a child's needs are met unpredictably, when caregivers are sometimes available and sometimes absent, the developing brain learns that the path to security is strict oversight and management. If your early world felt chaotic, if you couldn't predict whether care would arrive, your nervous system concluded that orchestrating everything was the only way to feel safe. That childhood adaptation becomes your adult operating system, long after the original threat has passed.

What worked as survival at seven becomes a trap at thirty-seven or fifty-seven. Samantha's mother had struggled with depression throughout Samantha's childhood. Some days bright and present, other days unreachable behind a closed bedroom door for hours or entire weekends. Young Samantha learned to read the signs, to handle her own needs quietly, to become responsible and reliable and in charge of the things she could manage since she couldn't control whether her mother would be okay. That same pattern, decades later, had her installing cameras in her father's house and tracking his medication in a spreadsheet. She was convinced that sufficient watchfulness could prevent loss, that if she just monitored carefully enough, she could stop the people she loved from disappearing the way her mother sometimes had. The mechanism that once helped her survive an unpredictable childhood was now destroying her relationship with her father.

The brain creates a comforting narrative when faced with uncertainty. If you just monitor more carefully, plan more thoroughly, intervene more quickly, you can manage outcomes that are inherently unmanageable. It's like trying to control the weather by checking the forecast obsessively, believing that attention itself creates influence. Technology feeds this delusion by making everything trackable. When you can monitor your aging parent's location in real time, review your children's grades through an app updated hourly, and check security cameras from your phone, your brain treats each piece of data as something requiring your coordination. The tools promise security but deliver only more anxiety, more things to track, and more variables demanding your oversight.

Contemporary culture mistakes this constant vigilance for virtue. Intensive parenting philosophies promise that with enough research and intervention, you can engineer perfect outcomes. Workplace expectations reward those who respond instantly to every notification, who remain perpetually available for crises, real or imagined. But somewhere in the gap between caring and controlling, something important gets lost. The dignity of the people you're trying to protect. The trust that forms the foundation of genuine relationship. The recognition that your surveillance doesn't prevent harm. It prevents the very connection you're trying to preserve.

Choosing to Release

Surrender emerges when you realize that your real power lies not in dictating what happens, but in choosing how you respond to whatever happens. When you choose surrender over control, you stop burning yourself out trying to orchestrate outcomes you cannot influence and start directing energy toward responses that genuinely matter. This requires distinguishing between influence and control. You have influence over your effort, attitude, preparation, and how you show up. You have control over almost nothing else. You cannot shape other people's decisions, the timing of opportunities, how circumstances unfold, or whether the people you love choose what you would choose.

Samantha experienced this shift when she finally asked her father a question she'd been avoiding. Not "Will you move to Meadowbrook?" but "What do you need from me?" His answer surprised her. Not more tracking or protocols or surveillance. He needed her to visit without an agenda, to call without interrogating him about medications, to trust he would ask for help when he needed it. He needed her to be his daughter instead of his case manager. Over the following months, she dismantled her apparatus slowly, keeping the medication app but checking it less compulsively. Removing the cameras and letting him handle his own routines. The transition was terrifying. What if something went wrong without constant oversight? Instead, something unexpected happened. Without her surveillance, her father seemed more alive, more engaged, and more like himself. He started cooking again, joined a community garden, seemed lighter somehow, like he'd been carrying the weight of her anxiety and had finally been allowed to set it down.

Their relationship changed too. Phone calls became conversations instead of interrogations. Visits became time together instead of inspections. She still worried, but the worry no longer drove every interaction. Psychologist Angela Duckworth, known for her work on grit, has found that people who remain passionate about long-term goals while staying flexible about the path achieve more with significantly less strain than those who try to control every variable.[17] They know when to persist and when to pivot, when to push and when to release. Surrender doesn't mean abandoning effort or care. It means pouring energy into what you can genuinely influence while releasing your grip on outcomes you cannot guarantee. Most importantly, it transforms uncertainty from enemy into reality, allowing you to show up for relationships rather than constantly trying to orchestrate them.

When Both Options Serve the Moment

Not all control deserves to be released, and not all surrender serves well-being. The art lies in recognizing what you can genuinely influence versus what you're depleting yourself trying to dictate. Some situations benefit from careful organization. When you're coordinating complex logistics or managing circumstances where you have direct influence, appropriate structure serves everyone involved. The distinction is whether your efforts increase your actual influence or simply increase your anxiety. Effective influence focuses on variables you can directly impact through your choices and actions. Ineffective control tries to orchestrate outcomes depending on other people's cooperation, timing you cannot determine, or factors beyond your reach.

Genuine concerns about well-being require different responses than anxiety-driven surveillance. If someone has dementia and cannot manage medications independently, appropriate protocols serve their safety. If they're cognitively intact but occasionally forget a dose, your elaborate tracking apparatus serves your anxiety more than their health. Time horizons matter too. Crisis situations often require temporary increased oversight and support. Someone recovering from surgery might need help with medications and daily tasks during healing. This differs fundamentally from permanent surveillance based on disasters that might possibly happen someday. The question is whether you're responding to actual present need or trying to prevent imagined future catastrophe.

Strategic structure helps when you're supporting someone as they build capacity or face complexity they cannot manage on their own. Surrender serves dignity and relationship when the outcome depends on another person's agency, on circumstances beyond anyone's control, or on situations where your grip creates dependence rather than support. Control that empowers looks like teaching someone to manage their own medication schedule. Control that suffocates looks like never giving them the chance to try. Support that trusts looks like being available when asked. Support shaped by anxiety looks like stepping into every decision, whether you're needed or not. The meta-skill isn't only about releasing control, it's about developing the wisdom to know when to act and when to trust, when to help, and when to honor agency.

Where This Choice Shows Up Every Day

Parenting Moments. Your teenager wants to handle college applications independently, and your hands itch to review every essay and manage every deadline. Control micromanages each step, convinced oversight prevents mistakes. Surrender teaches skills, stays available for questions, and trusts them to learn through their own process. They develop genuine competence instead of performative compliance.

Professional Settings. A team member approaches a project differently than you would, and panic rises about potential failure. Control redirects their work to match your vision, creating dependence and resentment. Surrender clarifies the outcome, offers support, and lets capable people contribute their strengths. The work improves, and you stop being the bottleneck.

Household Dynamics. You manage every schedule, chore, and decision because no one else does it your way. Control creates a household that runs on one person's exhaustion. Surrender invites shared ownership, teaches skills, and accepts that different approaches can still work. Others step up when given space, and you reclaim energy spent orchestrating everyone's movements.

Caregiving Relationships. Someone you love faces health challenges, and fear pushes you toward constant monitoring. Control adds systems, checks in obsessively, and treats them like a patient needing management. Surrender stays connected, offers help when asked, and honors their agency in their own life. The relationship deepens because care does not require surveillance.

Daily Life. Your carefully structured day hits unexpected obstacles, and frustration rises as plans shift. Control clings to the original schedule, turning disruptions into disasters. Surrender uses priorities as guides rather than mandates, adapts to what is actually happening, and finds steadiness in flexibility. The day becomes something you navigate rather than something that defeats you.

Practice Exercises: The GRACE Method

Control promises certainty but delivers exhaustion. These practices help you identify where you're gripping too tightly, recognize what's actually yours to shape, and experience the relief that comes when you stop trying to orchestrate outcomes you were never meant to direct.

G – Give yourself permission to release. Begin each morning by identifying one area where you tend to hold too tightly and intentionally loosen your grip for the day. Write a simple statement. "Today, I am not managing how the team discusses ideas." "Today I am not choreographing my partner's mood." Stating this aloud interrupts automatic control habits and primes your mind for a different way of operating.

R – Recognize your sphere of influence. When tension rises, draw a circle on paper. Write inside it only what you can directly shape through your choices: your preparation, communication, effort. Outside the circle, place what you cannot dictate: how others respond, timing of outcomes, whether plans unfold as you envisioned. Refocusing on what you can influence restores clarity and reduces the impulse to manage everything.

A – Accept what is without resistance. When reality shifts from your plans, practice saying, "This is what is happening right now." Say it with neutrality rather than judgment. "The project is running behind. This is what is happening right now." This allows your nervous system to settle so you can meet the moment as it is instead of battling how it should have been.

C – Choose your response consciously. Once acceptance settles, ask yourself, "What is the most skillful response available to me?" This question shifts you from fixing mode into wise response. Instead of forcing circumstances back into shape, you choose the next step that aligns with clarity, steadiness, and values.

E – Experience the freedom. Notice how your body responds when you stop trying to direct every outcome. Breathing deepens. Shoulders soften. Thinking becomes more spacious. This physical relief is evidence that surrender isn't failure but release from unnecessary strain. Let this sensation reinforce the truth that life becomes easier when you stop carrying what was never yours to control.

What Changes When You Stop

Samantha's father lived independently for three more years after she dismantled her apparatus. He fell once, a minor stumble in his garden resulting in a bruised hip. She received a phone call two hours after it happened instead of a camera alert. Her first instinct was to spiral back into control, to rebuild the protocols, to prove her watchfulness had been necessary all along. But her father's voice stopped her. Not scared. Not helpless. Just matter of fact. He'd fallen, gotten himself up, iced his hip. He was calling because he knew she'd want to know, not because he needed her to manage the situation. That phone call taught her what her spreadsheets never could. His dignity mattered more than her comfort. His agency mattered more than her certainty. That the relationship they'd built over those three years, based on trust rather than tracking, had been more valuable than any risk she'd prevented through monitoring.

When he did eventually need more help, when his health declined to where independent living was no longer viable, the conversation was different. Not her imposing a decision, but them making one together. Not her dictating his life, but him choosing to accept help he'd come to trust she would offer without conditions attached. Relationships deepen when you show up with presence rather than trying to coordinate every response. Personal peace emerges when you stop fighting reality and start engaging it. Most importantly, you develop genuine resilience, the ability to handle whatever emerges because you've stopped wasting energy trying to prevent emergence itself. The same intelligence you've been using to orchestrate outcomes could be redirected toward creating skillful responses to any outcome.

People trapped in constant monitoring report higher rates of anxiety, depression, and chronic stress. They damage relationships through micromanagement. They burn themselves out trying to guarantee results in an inherently uncertain world. The cost shows up everywhere. In bodies that can't relax. In relationships that feel like projects. In the exhaustion of carrying responsibility for outcomes beyond anyone's control. Your willingness to surrender control becomes the ground for peace and for genuine relationship, and it lets you see that people are often more capable than your fear suggests. Will you continue depleting yourself trying to orchestrate results you cannot influence, or will you discover the profound freedom that becomes available when you trust what you can influence and release what you cannot? The answer lives in your next choice to respond rather than control, to guide rather than guarantee, to trust rather than track.

6

Defend or Understand

the argument that wins nothing

Charles was carrying groceries out from the supermarket, bags balanced in both arms as he fumbled for his keys, when the text arrived. His 15-year-old daughter Sofia had stayed home sick from school, and he'd spent his lunch break picking up soup, crackers, and the specific brand of ginger ale she'd requested. Three stores to find it. He'd been the one to notice she preferred the glass bottles over cans because they "tasted better." He'd been paying attention. For three years since the divorce, he'd been paying attention in ways her mother never had. The early mornings sacrificed. Schedules rearranged without complaint. Monday's dentist appointment when she forgot to mention it until Sunday night. Wednesday's parent-teacher conference that conflicted with his department meeting. Six a.m. soccer practice every Saturday for three years, even the mornings after he'd worked late into the night. He'd been building his entire post-divorce identity around being the reliable parent, the one who showed up, the one who remembered glass bottles instead of cans.

"Dad where are you?? I needed you to sign my permission slip for the field trip next week and you're never here when I need you for anything important." Charles felt his chest collapse. Never here? The accusation landed exactly where it would hurt most. Every cell in his body started screaming in protest. He worked fifty hours a week to pay for her soccer, her phone, her everything. He couldn't read her mind about permission slips. His thumbs moved across the screen before his breathing caught up to his thinking. "Are you kidding me right now? I'm literally at the store buying you soup because you're sick. I work 50 hours a week to pay for everything, and this is the thanks I get? I can't read your mind. Maybe try telling me about things more than 12 hours before they're due." He hit send and immediately felt the surge of being right. There. Now she'd understand how unfair she was being. Now she'd appreciate everything he did instead of fixating on the one thing he'd missed. His evidence was airtight. His defense was logical. His position was reasonable.

The response came back within seconds. "Whatever Dad. Forget it. I'll just miss the trip." That was it. No acknowledgment of his points. No apology. Just dismissal and guilt manipulation. Charles stood still, groceries growing heavy in his arms, feeling something sharp settle into his stomach. He'd won the argument. His points were valid, his defense was logical, his position was reasonable. So why did winning suddenly feel like losing? He could already see how the day would unfold. He'd walk inside ready to continue making his case. She'd give him one-word answers from behind her phone. The gap between what he'd been trying to show her and what she'd been trying to tell him would widen with every defensive word he prepared.

Sofia was curled up on the couch, her fever-flushed face wet with tears that had nothing to do with being sick. She'd been looking forward to the museum trip for weeks. It was the first fun thing that had happened at school since her friend group had imploded over drama she still didn't fully understand. Her dad was always busy, always stressed, always explaining himself instead of just being there. She hadn't meant to sound accusatory. She'd been panicking about missing another thing, feeling disconnected from him, wishing he could somehow know what she needed without her having to explain everything. But now he was angry at her for needing him, and she felt even more alone. Every time she tried to tell him she needed him more present, he heard it as criticism of how hard he was working. Every time he listed everything he did for her, she heard that his efforts mattered more than her feelings.

Charles walked inside armed with counterarguments and wounded pride. Sofia was about to retreat further into the shell that protected her from feeling like a burden on the person she needed most. Neither of them realized they were fighting about completely different things. Neither of them saw that every point Charles won pushed Sofia further away. He was defending his devotion. She was asking to feel connected. The groceries he'd bought with such care sat forgotten in the driveway, exactly like the connection between them.

Why Your Choice Matters

You can win every argument and still lose every relationship that matters. Most arguments aren't about who's right and who's wrong. They're about two people having different experiences that could be bridged through inquiry rather than demolished through defense. Your partner criticizes your driving and you immediately launch into justifying your fourteen-year accident-free record. A colleague questions your project approach and you respond with detailed explanations of why their concerns don't apply instead of asking what they're seeing. Your teenager expresses frustration and you hear personal attack instead of adolescent overwhelm. This is the moment when you choose between defending and understanding, two fundamentally different responses to feeling challenged that most people navigate unconsciously dozens of times per day.

Defending feels natural and necessary, proof that you have self-respect. When someone questions your choices, criticizes your actions, or challenges your perspective, every instinct screams that you need to protect yourself, prove your point, and secure your position. Your reputation is at stake. Your competence is being questioned. Your worth feels under attack. Psychologist John Gottman's research on relationship dynamics reveals the devastating pattern.[18] Habitual defending transforms every disagreement into a competition where somebody has to be right and somebody has to be wrong, somebody wins and somebody loses. Couples who respond to complaints with defensiveness are significantly more likely to divorce than those who respond with curiosity. Defending is one of Gottman's Four Horsemen, reliably predicting relationship failure across thousands of couples studied over decades. You're not protecting your relationship when you defend yourself. You're slowly dismantling it.

Understanding feels dangerous when you're feeling attacked. It sounds like admitting fault, accepting blame, or giving the other person ammunition to use against you. You worry that if you don't protect your position, you'll be seen as weak, wrong, or incompetent. That if you show openness about their perspective, you're validating their criticism and invalidating your own experience. But understanding operates from a radically different premise. You can be completely right about your intentions and still learn something valuable from someone else's experience of your impact. You're bracing against the very person trying to understand you. Most conflicts arise not from malicious intent but from different perspectives, needs, or information that could be bridged through inquiry.

The defending mind treats every challenge as an attack that must be repelled. The understanding mind treats every challenge as information that might contain something valuable, even when it's delivered poorly.

Why We Launch into Defense

When someone questions your choices or challenges your perspective, Wharton professor and best-selling author Adam Grant's research on organizational psychology suggests that many people shift into what he calls preacher or prosecutor mode, focusing on defending views and winning the argument rather than understanding.[19] This mode can feel productive, but you are focused on how to win, not how to understand. When you stay in this argument mode, you experience what researchers call cognitive entrenchment, a rigid pattern of thinking that makes you increasingly committed to your existing position even in the face of disconfirming evidence. The more you argue for your position, the more committed you become to it, even when presented with evidence that suggests a different approach might serve you better. Your brain treats changing your mind as losing, so you dig in deeper rather than getting curious about what you might be missing.

This pattern took root when protecting yourself actually kept you safe. Maybe a parent responded to your mistakes with disappointment that felt like withdrawal of love. Maybe admitting fault in your family meant endless lectures or becoming the identified problem. Maybe you learned that the safest response to criticism was an immediate counterargument that shifted attention away from your vulnerability. If expressing needs led to criticism or vulnerability meant getting hurt, you developed reflexes designed to shield you from experiencing that pain again. When criticism touched areas connected to your sense of competence, whether that was parenting, work performance, or relationship skills, your system learned to treat it as a challenge to your fundamental adequacy as a person. You weren't just defending a specific choice. You were protecting your worth as a capable human being.

You rarely notice when this reflex becomes your default because it feels like something else entirely. Standing up for yourself feels righteous. Refusing to accept unfair accusations feels principled. Correcting misconceptions feels responsible. You tell yourself you are being accurate, fair, reasonable. But research on conflict and communication shows that people who mostly defend and advocate for their own position, without genuine inquiry into others' perspectives, tend to experience more relationship strain, workplace tension, and social disconnection than those who balance advocacy with inquiry. When your teenager says they need you, your nervous system might interpret it as an accusation because historically, being needed has meant being blamed. Charles's defensiveness was never about the permission slip. It was about protecting himself from feeling like he was failing as a father. The pattern that once sheltered you now prevents the very connection you are trying so hard to receive. Most people spend their lives waiting to feel understood while refusing to understand anyone else first.

Discerning Your Blind Spots

Understanding emerges when you see that impact and intention rarely align, and that someone's experience often lives in the space between. This single recognition changes everything. When you choose understand over defend, you transform from someone who needs to be right into someone who wants to be connected. You stop treating disagreements as zero-sum exchanges where one person's validity requires the other person's invalidation. You can maintain full confidence in your intentions while genuinely investigating how those intentions landed in someone else's experience. The person challenging you might be the only one who cares enough to risk your reaction.

Business theorist Chris Argyris examined how people learn and reason inside organizations and discovered that understanding creates what he called "double-loop learning," the ability to examine not just what went wrong but also why your approach might have contributed to unintended outcomes.[20] Single-loop learning asks how to be more right next time. Double-loop learning asks what assumptions led you to approach the situation the way you did. This leads to genuine improvement rather than more compelling arguments about why things went wrong. Understanding asks different questions than defending. Instead of asking how their criticism is unfair, it wonders what they might be experiencing that you are not seeing. Instead of asking how you can prove your point, it asks what their perspective might reveal.

Charles discovered this possibility when he walked inside and found Sofia crying on the couch. His first instinct was to continue defending his position, to explain again how much he did for her and how unfair her criticism felt. But seeing her tears, something in him shifted. "Sof, I am obviously missing something here. Can you help me understand what is really going on?" What emerged was that Sofia was not criticizing his availability. She was overwhelmed by school stress, friend drama, and feeling like she could not keep track of everything happening in her life. The permission slip was only the trigger for larger feelings she did not know how to articulate. She felt guilty asking for help because she could see how tired he was. He believed providing for her demonstrated love, but she was craving emotional presence more than financial support. Neither position was wrong. Both were incomplete. Understanding revealed what defense had been blocking.

When Both Options Serve the Moment

Sometimes defending serves you. When someone attacks your character rather than discussing specific behaviors, or when criticism becomes personal abuse, assertive self-advocacy protects your well-being and communicates your limits clearly. The key distinction is whether you are responding to genuine attack or to perceived threat. Actual attacks on your worth, dignity, or safety call for clear and firm responses that establish boundaries without escalation. But most of what feels like attack is actually something else. Criticism, concern, different perspectives, and poorly communicated needs often benefit more from curiosity than from counterargument. The person who learns to tell the difference stops exhausting themselves in battles that were never actually fights.

Understanding serves connection when someone's concern might contain useful information, when relationship dynamics need exploration, or when conflicts arise from miscommunication rather than true incompatibility. Approaching disagreements with openness often reveals solutions that self-protection obscures. But understanding becomes problematic when it turns into people-pleasing, accepting inappropriate behavior, or abandoning your own needs to avoid conflict. Healthy understanding maintains your boundaries while remaining genuinely receptive to another person's experience. What feels like criticism in the moment often reveals itself as care expressed clumsily. What seems like attack often turns out to be overwhelm, fear, or unmet needs taking whatever form they can to be noticed.

The question is not whether to defend or understand is better. The question is what the moment actually calls for. Clear self-protection honors your dignity when disrespect appears. Understanding builds connection when a difference in perspective can be bridged through mutual curiosity.

Most people default to protection when openness would serve them better. They treat every challenge as threat, every question as accusation, every concern as criticism. What changes is your ability to feel challenged without feeling threatened, and questioned without feeling accused. The meta-skill isn't just about managing conflict, it's about learning to feel challenged without feeling threatened, and being questioned without feeling accused.

Where This Choice Shows Up Every Day

Parenting Moments. Your teenager challenges your rules, boundaries, or understanding of their world. Defend jumps in to explain why your expectations make sense and why their reaction feels unreasonable. Understand pays attention to the need beneath their resistance and explores how the family dynamic might work better for everyone involved.

Partnerships. Your partner expresses frustration about communication, shared responsibilities, or emotional availability. Defend immediately lists everything you contribute and why their complaint feels off. Understand becomes curious about their experience and works with them to identify what would create more connection and ease.

Professional Settings. A colleague questions your approach, timeline, or assumptions in a meeting. Defend focuses on reinforcing your reasoning and dismissing their concerns. Understand considers what they might be seeing that you have not noticed and uses their input to strengthen the project.

Family Dynamics. A relative comments on your choices, priorities, or lifestyle during a gathering. Defend starts justifying your decisions and mentally noting all the ways they misunderstand you. Understand looks for the intention or worry behind their comment and takes whatever insight is useful without absorbing the judgment.

Friendship Conflicts. A friend questions a decision you made that affects them, like canceling a trip you planned together, missing an important event, or changing plans without discussion. Defend focuses on why your choice was necessary and justified given your circumstances. Understand acknowledges the impact on them first, stays present with their disappointment, and works through what the friendship needs without prioritizing your reasoning over their experience.

Practice Exercises: The Line of Inquiry

Defensiveness happens faster than thought. These practices help you slow the reaction down, recognize what you're actually protecting, and choose whether the argument you're about to have is worth more than the relationship you're trying to keep.

What am I trying to protect? Most defensiveness begins with a wound, not a disagreement. You may be protecting your competence, your integrity, your belonging, or your sense of being a good parent, partner, or professional. When you name what feels threatened, the moment starts making sense. The reaction that seemed automatic reveals itself as a strategy. And strategies can be changed.

What is actually at risk? Your nervous system reacts as if everything is at stake, but it rarely is. This question breaks the spell of urgency and shrinks the threat down to its real size. Often, the only thing at risk is pride. Sometimes it is simply the discomfort of hearing something you would rather not hear. When you see the true stakes clearly, the impulse to defend often softens on its own.

What matters more right now, this argument or this relationship? Arguments end. Relationships either deepen or erode. You can prove every point and still harm something that matters far more than winning. This question pulls you out of the heat of the moment and restores perspective. Most people protect their position by default, then wonder why closeness keeps slipping away.

What might be true in their experience, even if I disagree? Understanding does not require agreement. You can fully hear someone's perspective without abandoning your own. This question opens space in conversations that feel airless. It signals to the other person that you are willing to listen, and it signals to your own nervous system that you are steady enough to take in new information without losing yourself.

What would I say if I wasn't afraid? Fear distorts clarity. It makes honest and tender expression feel dangerous, so you default to sharp or guarded instead. This question brings you back to your core values. Honesty, courage, vulnerability, integrity. It anchors the moment in who you want to be rather than who the situation is tempting you to become.

What You Find When the Argument Stops

When Charles shifted from defending his parenting to understanding Sofia's experience, their relationship changed. She began sharing more about school stress because she no longer had to worry that her concerns would be interpreted as criticism. He discovered that his daughter did not need him to be perfect. She needed him to be present and curious about her world. Their next conflict, when Sofia wanted to quit soccer after three years, began with Charles's familiar instinct to defend the investment he had made in early morning practices and long weekends at tournaments. But instead of arguing about wasted time and commitment, he asked what was happening that made her want to quit. The team dynamics had become toxic, and Sofia was trying to protect her mental health. The conversation that followed revealed solutions neither of them would have found through argument.

Each time you choose understand over defend, you create space for genuine connection to grow where conflict once lived. This choice determines whether disagreements turn into power struggles that leave everyone feeling unheard, or into conversations that deepen understanding and strengthen relationships. The cost of habitual defending is quiet isolation. People who protect themselves by default often feel misunderstood, unsupported, and constantly on guard. They rarely see how their own patterns block the connection and appreciation they are longing for. They win arguments but lose closeness. They prove their points but miss openings for learning and mutual support. Every victory pushes someone further away.

You develop what might be called relational capacity, the ability to navigate differences without sacrificing either connection or authenticity. You become someone who can hold your own perspective while genuinely learning from others, someone who can stay grounded in your values while remaining open to what another person's experience might show you. The people in your life are not opponents in a debate. They are partners in learning how to live and work and love one another more effectively. The person you have been protecting yourself against might be the one trying hardest to reach you. Your willingness to understand rather than defend becomes the foundation for every authentic relationship you build, every conflict you resolve without casualties, and every moment when connection matters more than being right.

7

Envy or Admire

the mirror that you distort

Rachel was scrolling through Facebook at 4:23 p.m. when her mother's post appeared. Her younger sister Lena stood in front of a corporate banner, sharp navy blazer, smile radiant. The caption was pure maternal pride. "SO PROUD OF MY LENA!!! Promoted to Executive Vice President, youngest person ever to hold this position at her company! All those years of hard work are paying off!" Rachel's jaw clenched before she could stop it. The post already had sixty-two likes. Comments poured in from relatives and family friends, each one landing with a familiar sting. Her phone buzzed with a group text from her mother seconds later. "Family dinner Sunday to celebrate Lena! Can't wait to see everyone!" Rachel set her phone down and stared at her computer screen, her mind suddenly blank. Sunday. She had four days before she would have to sit at that table with a smile she couldn't hold.

By Thursday night, her shoulders were already tight. She found herself rehearsing congratulations in the bathroom mirror, watching her reflection carefully, adjusting the smile until it looked like something that might pass for genuine happiness. The tightness in her chest wouldn't ease. By Friday morning, Rachel had scrolled through Lena's LinkedIn profile three times. MBA, CPA, Six Sigma certification. Each credential felt like another metric she was quietly tallying, even if she couldn't admit what she was measuring. Lena was Executive Vice President at 32. Rachel was still a program director at 34, doing work she'd always said mattered more than titles. Every time she pictured Sunday dinner, her stomach dropped. Not because she didn't love her sister, but because she couldn't separate Lena's success from the rising fear that she had fallen behind in ways she hadn't let herself acknowledge.

Sunday arrived carrying the weight she had felt building all week. She stood in her mother's kitchen holding the expensive wine she'd bought, watching Lena show their mother photos on her phone. Both of them laughing at something Rachel had missed. Lena looked up and crossed the room with arms open. Rachel returned the hug, careful not to hold herself so stiffly that it revealed how small she felt standing next to her younger sister's growing world. "I still can't believe this is real," Lena said quietly against her shoulder. "I keep waiting for them to realize they made a mistake." The modesty sounded genuine. It probably was.

Their mother called everyone to the table. The conversation turned immediately to Lena's promotion. Questions about her new role, the size of her team, what the board had said during the announcement. Genuine celebration filled the room while Rachel's chest tightened with each detail and each proud glance their mother offered Lena. She heard herself offering congratulations that sounded hollow in her own ears. Felt her face holding an expression that required conscious effort to maintain. Her mind was already assembling reasons why this was different, why Lena's path had been easier, why this successful moment meant less than everyone believed it did. Anything to stop it from feeling like her sister's achievement was illuminating a gap Rachel didn't want to see.

She could spend the entire evening building that story. Finding every explanation that would shrink what Lena had earned until it stopped threatening the narrative she relied on about choosing meaningful work over ambition. Or she could sit with the uncomfortable truth her envy was revealing. Lena's success wasn't stealing anything from her. It was pointing toward a question she had been avoiding. If she truly believed her nonprofit work mattered more than titles, if she genuinely didn't need recognition or advancement to feel fulfilled, then why did watching her younger sister succeed make her feel the absence of something she had convinced herself she didn't want?

Why Your Choice Matters

Someone else's success changes nothing about your capacity. But it feels like it changes everything. Your colleague gets the promotion, and suddenly your accomplishments feel smaller. Your friend buys the house, and your apartment feels inadequate. Your sister becomes Executive Vice President, and the work you chose feels like the work you settled for. Nothing about your actual life shifted. But everything about how you experience your life just tilted. The person who succeeded didn't diminish you. But envy distorts the mirror until it looks like they did. It turns their gain into your inadequacy, their achievement into evidence of your failure, their expansion into proof of your limits. You can let their success corrode you, or you can let it illuminate what's possible.

Envy works like a lens that bends someone else's reality into a version that highlights your inadequacy. Their success becomes evidence of your failure. Their ease becomes proof of your struggle. Their visibility becomes confirmation of your invisibility. You start cataloging their advantages. Better connections, more support, fewer obstacles, natural talents you'll never possess. The list grows more detailed until the distorted reflection feels more real than what's actually in front of you. Sonja Lyubomirsky, a social psychologist who studies happiness and well-being, has shown that frequent social comparison is one of the fastest ways to erode happiness.[21] Her research on social comparison reveals the mechanism driving this distortion. When you compare yourself to others, your brain doesn't evaluate objective reality. It evaluates relative position. You're not measuring whether your life is good. You're measuring whether your life is better or worse than theirs. This creates upward social comparison, measuring yourself against people who appear more successful. The comparison doesn't motivate improvement. It just makes you feel inadequate while changing nothing.

Envy keeps you cataloging what they have while building nothing of your own. The energy spent tallying their advantages could develop your capabilities. The time spent explaining why their path was easier could be spent walking your own. Envy offers something seductive in exchange for all that lost momentum. It protects you from the vulnerability of wanting something badly enough to pursue it. If their success is illegitimate because of advantages you lack, then your lack of success is not really about you. The story you build becomes protection against the more unsettling truth that you could pursue what you want but have been too afraid to try. Admiration offers a different path. It looks at someone else's achievement and asks what it reveals about possibility rather than what it proves about what you lack. It studies approaches instead of cataloging advantages. It lets their success expand your sense of what is achievable instead of contracting your sense of worth. Someone else's win is not a referendum on your adequacy. It is information about paths you did not know existed. Their expansion does not require your contraction.

Why We Turn Comparison Into Identity

When someone else succeeds, your mind turns their news into a story about you. It immediately evaluates your position relative to theirs and generates a verdict about your worth. This response runs automatically because your nervous system evolved to track social standing within groups where rank determined survival. Alfred Adler, an early 20th-century psychiatrist and founder of individual psychology, argued that people develop their sense of self through comparing themselves with others and forming what he called feelings of inferiority that fuel lifelong striving.[22] This wasn't neurosis. It was adaptation. That ancient wiring misfires constantly now. You're no longer assessing a handful of tribe members whose full lives you witnessed. You're measuring yourself against thousands of strangers who exist only as achievement announcements, each one landing as evidence of where you fall short. What once protected you now quietly diminishes you, one comparison at a time.

Digital platforms don't just enable comparison. They're built to amplify it. Social media algorithms curate content to show you people slightly ahead of where you are, the zone most likely to trigger engagement through envy. You see their promotion announcement without the years of rejection that came before. Their dream home without the inheritance or debt behind it. Their thriving relationship without the therapy that holds it together. The algorithm feeds you polished outcomes stripped of struggle, then your brain runs its ancient program. It calculates your position, measures the gap, and concludes you're falling behind. Achievement becomes performance staged for an audience that never stops watching. Your worth gets determined not by what you build but by how you measure against what everyone else is building bigger and faster and louder. Research shows this constant exposure correlates with depression, anxiety, and decreased life satisfaction.[23] The technology promising connection delivers the opposite. It delivers isolation disguised as community.

Envy persists because it protects you from something harder to face than inadequacy. It protects you from wanting. If you can catalog their advantages, you don't have to confront your own hunger for what they've claimed. If their success required circumstances you lack, your absence of success doesn't reflect on your capability. The protection holds. This mechanism intensifies in relationships where identity formed through contrast. When the sibling everyone called steady becomes wildly successful, or the friend who always struggled suddenly thrives, the ground shifts. Their transformation doesn't just challenge your assumptions. It threatens the entire story about who you are and what remains possible for you. The envy you feel isn't really about them. It's about recognizing that if they can rewrite their script, you've been performing a role that was never actually permanent.

From Inventory to Insight

Rachel sat at her mother's dinner table surrounded by happiness she couldn't feel and caught herself mid-spiral. Her mind was compiling reasons why Lena's path had been smoother, explaining away the success that made her feel inadequate. But this time she paused. She asked herself a different question. What if my sister's achievement isn't diminishing me? What if it's showing me something I've been afraid to want? The answer arrived with uncomfortable clarity. She'd been using her nonprofit work as proof that she valued mission over ambition, but watching Lena claim executive leadership revealed the lie. Rachel wanted influence too. She wanted her work to reach further. Lena's promotion wasn't stealing anything. It was illuminating a desire Rachel had buried under explanations about why other paths weren't for her.

Social neuroscientist Tania Singer's research on empathy reveals the distinction between witnessing someone else's experience and making it about your own.[24] When you observe another person's success without translating it into your inadequacy, comparison stops distorting what you see. The shift happens when you stop asking why they succeeded and start asking what their path reveals about possibilities you haven't explored. Admiration becomes inquiry. Instead of itemizing the advantages that make their success illegitimate, you study the approach that made it possible. Someone building a career you admire doesn't have resources you lack, they have choices you haven't made. Their expansion doesn't contract your possibility. It reveals options you've been dismissing.

This shift began showing up everywhere once Rachel knew how to notice it. When a colleague received recognition, she felt the familiar tightening, then wondered what his visibility revealed about ways she might be keeping herself small. When a friend shared travel photos, she noticed the envy, then became curious about whether adventure actually mattered to her. When scrolling pulled her into comparison, she practiced asking what each moment was pointing toward in her own unexplored desires. The work was never about eliminating envy. It was about catching the distortion before it turned someone else's reality into evidence of her limitation. Each time she chose to see achievement as information rather than indictment, the distortion eased.

When Both Options Serve the Moment

Some moments genuinely stir envy in ways that deserve attention rather than judgment. Another person's achievement exposes a longing you have ignored or postponed. The pang you feel is not a flaw. It is information revealing the gap between the life you are living and the life you still want to claim. In these moments envy serves you because it points toward a desire you have not honored. It shows you dreams you buried, paths you abandoned, or parts of yourself you have not allowed room to grow. It brings into focus the places where your life feels smaller than your deeper desires. Envy becomes a signal that you are ready for a different conversation with your own life. The discomfort becomes direction. The ache becomes invitation.

And there are moments when envy shifts, not because the feeling is wrong, but because the meaning you attach to it begins to narrow your view. What starts as longing turns into a quiet judgment of your own worth. Someone else's success feels like a subtraction from your life rather than a reminder of what is possible. The comparison tightens your focus until you lose sight of the truth of your own path. The work is not to eliminate envy, but to understand what story it is protecting. The fear of wanting too much. The fear of failing if you try. The fear that your life should be further along by now. These fears do not erase the longing. They simply show you where clarity is needed before desire can become movement.

Admiration becomes essential when you are ready to respond from truth rather than protection. It doesn't ask you to pretend success is easy for others or painless for you. It simply shifts the meaning you make of it. Admiration recognizes another person's growth without turning it into commentary on your worth. It acknowledges the beauty in someone else's expansion and lets that expansion point you toward your own. It creates space for compassion, humility, and strength all at once. It keeps you rooted in your own unfolding rather than tangled in someone else's story. The meta-skill is not choosing between envy and admire. It's developing the capacity to let another person's life awaken your own without losing yourself in the comparison.

Where This Choice Shows Up Every Day

Friendships. Your friend posts keys to her first home and your rental suddenly feels insufficient. Envy creates distance. You delay responding to her messages, convinced her progress exposes something lacking in your own life. Admire keeps you grounded. You text congratulations, ask about her journey, and let her achievement clarify whether homeownership matters to you at all.

Workplaces. A colleague gets the promotion you wanted and your stomach drops when you see the announcement. Envy makes you second-guess your presence in the next meeting, convinced their advancement says something definitive about your worth. Admire shifts the lens. You study what made them visible, consider what skills would strengthen your own trajectory, and let their success clarify what is possible in your environment.

Intimate Relationships. Your partner launches a business while your career feels stagnant, and suddenly everything they share stirs comparison. Envy turns their wins into quiet measurement. You pull back or find reasons to dismiss their choices. Admire lets you name what their momentum stirs in you. You celebrate their expansion, and the honesty deepens connection instead of creating distance.

Daily Life. You scroll past an announcement and your chest tightens before you even register what triggered it. Envy wants to list what they have that you do not. Admire pauses long enough to ask what your reaction reveals about your own unnamed desires, then moves on without letting their story overwrite yours.

Family Dynamics. Your younger sister gets engaged and you feel yourself fading into the background. Envy revives old hierarchies, convincing you her milestone diminishes your place. Admire recognizes the ache without letting it speak for you. You offer genuine congratulations, ask about what matters to her, and let the moment surface questions about what you actually want.

Practice Exercises: The Decoder Sequence

Envy arrives as comparison but carries information about what you want. These practices help you decode the signal before it becomes self-criticism, separate what you're actually envying from what you're seeing, and turn the discomfort into movement toward what matters to you.

Question. When envy hits, ask what it is showing you that you want. Don't analyze. Don't compare. Just name it. Their promotion might reflect a desire for visibility. Their relationship might reveal a desire for partnership. Their travel might surface a desire for freedom. The question decodes envy's signal before it becomes noise.

Separation. Notice what you are comparing. Their highlight against your struggle. Their finished product against your messy process. Their curated moment against your unfiltered experience. You are not comparing equal realities. The comparison collapses when you see the asymmetry. You are envying their edited version while judging your rough draft.

Translation. Get specific about what you actually want. Not *I want what they have*, but the hunger underneath. Is it influence, creative expression, freedom, recognition, adventure, security? Write it in one sentence without their name appearing anywhere. Their name disappears. Your truth moves to the center. Envy loses power when it stops being about them and becomes clarity about you.

Study. Study the choices that shaped their success, not the advantages that made it easier. What did they risk? What did they practice? What did they prioritize or release? Progress comes from decisions you can also make, not from circumstances you cannot control. Admiration studies choices. Envy watches advantages. One opens possibility. The other confirms limitation.

Move. Within five minutes, do one small thing that aligns with what you want. Text someone about an opportunity. Research a skill you need. Draft a paragraph. Book the appointment you have been postponing. The timeline matters because motion interrupts the distortion before it takes hold. You stop consuming someone else's life and start creating movement in your own. Action breaks the spell that comparison casts.

When Comparison Becomes Clarity

Six months after that dinner table conversation, Lena was promoted again. This time she called Rachel first, not to manage her sister's reaction but to share news that mattered. Rachel congratulated her. They talked about what the role would require, what frightened Lena about it, and what excited her. The call lasted twelve minutes, and neither of them was performing. A month later, Rachel landed a client she had been pursuing for a year. Lena texted immediately, asked about the pitch, celebrated the win. The comparison that once colored their relationship had softened into curiosity about each other's actual lives. They no longer used one another's successes as commentary on their own.

Rachel discovered that envy had not vanished. It still surfaced when she scrolled past achievements that brushed against her own insecurities. But now it arrived as a signal rather than a conclusion. When comparison tightened her chest, she asked what it revealed about desires she had not honored. Some moments pointed toward paths she wanted to explore. Others simply reminded her that every life looks curated from the outside and complicated from within. She could notice someone else's win without measuring her worth against it. The distortion eased when she stopped treating it as a singular truth.

Every time you choose admire over envy, you teach yourself that another person's success reveals possibility rather than inadequacy. This choice shapes whether comparison narrows or expands your world. Whether relationships deepen through celebration or strain under competition. Whether you invest your energy tracking advantages you lack or strengthening capacities you already possess. The shift is not dramatic. It's steady. Someone gets the promotion, finds the partner, launches the business, and instead of feeling smaller, you feel curious. You stop asking why them and begin asking what the moment is showing you about what you want.

You begin developing what can be called clarity of vision, the ability to witness another person's expansion without losing sight of your own. Professional opportunities multiply because you study what works rather than watch what feels unfair. Relationships deepen because you celebrate rather than compete. Personal growth accelerates when you let others' successes illuminate your desires rather than confirming your limitations. Your sense of yourself was never distorted by their achievement. It was shaped by the meaning you attached to it. The person who learns to separate these discovers something different than relief. They discover freedom. Someone else's expansion does not require your contraction. You can witness their growth and remain rooted in your own unfolding. The question becomes whether you will keep standing in front of the funhouse mirror waiting for your reflection to change, or whether you will step away and see clearly what has been yours all along.

8

Judgment or Curiosity

the gavel that silences wonder

Stephanie's wine glass stalled midair as laughter erupted from the kitchen. The kind of laughter she had not heard from her daughter in years. Not the polite, brittle chuckle Olivia had offered all evening, but the kind that comes from shared jokes and easy familiarity. The kind Stephanie had spent three years trying to build with her daughter and never quite reached. She sat at the dining table pretending to check her phone, but really she was listening. Noting every detail. Beginning the case she had been assembling since Olivia walked through the door with Brandon, holding his hand like he belonged there. Twenty-three years old and bringing home someone who wore a vintage Radiohead T-shirt to meet her mother, who arrived with craft beer instead of wine, who called her Steph instead of Ms. Warren.

She could hear Brandon from the kitchen. "Your mom's intense, huh?" Stephanie's stomach dropped. Her hands went cold around her phone. Olivia's response came next, softer but unmistakable. "Always has been. She means well, but…" The rest disappeared under running water, but Stephanie heard the tone. Apologetic. Cautious. Her jaw tightened until her molars ached. That familiar surge rose in her chest, part hurt and part righteous certainty, the mixture that had fueled every difficult conversation with her daughter for a decade. She was not being intense. She was being a mother. She had spent Olivia's entire childhood making sure her daughter had every advantage she never had. Private violin lessons paid for by double shifts. Months of research before every SAT prep decision. And this was the result. Being quietly dissected in her own kitchen by a boy who did not even know you were supposed to dress up for dinner.

The water shut off. The laughter faded. Stephanie's shoulders tensed as she heard them moving through the kitchen, voices dropping to whispers. Her breath went shallow. That prickling behind her eyes started, the one that always came right before she said something she could not take back. The college visit when she had pointed out that Olivia's first-choice school was not really a reach school, and Olivia barely spoke the whole drive home. The interview last year when Stephanie questioned the company's financial stability, and Olivia snapped that not everything needed analyzing to death. Every observation had been meant to help. Every suggestion offered with care. Every piece of feedback designed to protect Olivia from mistakes Stephanie had learned the hard way. Yet somehow each one had pushed her daughter further away.

They walked into the dining room wearing that careful brightness people use after they have been talking about you. Olivia's smile was too wide. Brandon looked like he wanted to disappear. "Mom, Brandon and I are going to head out." Olivia's voice carried the neutral tone she used when working hard not to fight. "Thanks for dinner." The words Stephanie had been composing all evening crowded behind her teeth. The comment about how they had only been here two hours. The remark about appreciation. She opened her mouth and saw the look in Olivia's eyes. That weary, preemptive brace. Ready for criticism. Already preparing explanations. Already calculating whether this would be the visit that ended with weeks of silence.

The words were right there. Sharp. Justified. Familiar. She could feel the pattern taking over, the one where she said what needed saying and Olivia retreated, and Stephanie comforted herself by believing that someday her daughter would understand she had only been trying to help. Except maybe Olivia would never understand because Stephanie had spent so many years being right that she had forgotten how to be close. The observations felt accurate. The judgment felt earned. But she suddenly saw, with painful clarity, that her version of love had become a place where Olivia always felt evaluated. And what that evaluation had created was distance neither of them wanted.

Why Your Choice Matters

You've confused judgment with engagement. You offer observations, corrections you cannot hold back, and suggestions meant to be helpful, believing they show how much you care. The sharper your eye for what needs improvement, the more it feels as if you are expressing love through vigilance. You notice what others miss because you are paying attention. You point out potential problems because you are thinking ahead. You offer unsolicited feedback because someone needs to be honest. This feels like devotion. Like protection. Like the kind of love that refuses to let people stumble when you can already see where they are about to fall. The more you care, the more intensely you assess what is happening around you. The logic feels airtight.

But the people receiving this constant scrutiny experience something entirely different. They feel measured against standards they never agreed to and examined in moments that should have been simple. They begin to anticipate being corrected and brace for critique even in ordinary conversations. Your judgment does not feel like care to them. It feels like living under watchful eyes, where nothing they do will ever feel quite enough. The distance between you grows with every helpful observation, every gentle correction, every moment you choose being right over being close. They stop sharing what matters because they have learned that sharing means being judged, and being judged means being found insufficient in ways you will inevitably name.

Clinical psychologist Harriet Lerner spent decades studying how criticism operates in relationships, and her findings challenge everything most people believe about honest feedback.[25] Her research shows that chronic criticism does more than damage connection. It quietly dismantles it. The person offering critiques believes they are being supportive and truthful about what needs improvement. The person receiving them experiences something far more discouraging. They begin to feel that nothing about them is acceptable as it is. Lerner's work reveals a difficult truth. You can be completely right about what needs to change and completely wrong about whether naming it strengthens the relationship. The standards you held became the space between you. The bar you raised with good intentions became the barrier preventing genuine connection.

Every time you judge instead of explore, you choose your sense of correctness over the other person's actual experience. You think you are preventing mistakes, but you're actually preventing intimacy. The people in your life do not need your constant critique. They need your curiosity about who they are when they are not being sized up. And the more you judge, the less they share. The less they share, the more your conclusions rest on fragments and guesses. You build a system where your confidence grows even as your understanding shrinks, where you feel increasingly certain while knowing less and less.

Curiosity offers something entirely different. It approaches the same moments with genuine interest rather than judgment. When someone makes a choice that baffles you, judgment catalogs what is wrong with it. Curiosity asks what makes perfect sense from where they are standing. This shift is not about lowering your standards. It is about recognizing that your certainty about what is right for someone else may be far less reliable than your willingness to understand what is true for them. Most of what you judge is not harmful. It is simply different from how you would do it.

Why We Mistake Criticism for Care

When judgment became your default, it wasn't arbitrary or mean-spirited. It formed in environments where alertness kept you safe and high standards protected you from consequences you could not afford. Maybe you grew up in a home where mistakes were met with disappointment that felt like withdrawal of love, where pointing out problems before they escalated was the only way to prevent explosions you had no power to stop. Maybe you learned early that the world punishes carelessness and that nobody was going to shield you from its impact. Developing a sharp eye for what could go wrong became a way to stay ahead of trouble. The critical lens you learned was the only protection you had. It became competence shaped by circumstances where being right mattered more than being close, because closeness did not guarantee safety and accuracy sometimes did.

Melanie Klein, a pioneering psychoanalyst in object relations theory, described how people cope with anxiety by splitting their experience into "good" and "bad" parts and then projecting the unwanted parts onto others.[26] Her work on splitting explains how people manage anxiety by dividing the world into categories that feel controllable. Good and bad. Right and wrong. Acceptable and unacceptable. When life feels overwhelming, these categories offer structure. But Klein found that this mechanism does more than organize the external world. It organizes your internal one too. The parts of yourself that don't meet your own standards often get projected onto other people, then criticized there. When Stephanie judges Brandon's casual approach, she is not simply reacting to him. She is rejecting the part of herself that longed to be less rigid and less exhausting in her pursuit of doing everything right. The judgment appears to be about him. It is actually about the anxiety she cannot tolerate in herself.

This pattern intensifies in relationships where you have sacrificed enormously. When you have worked double shifts so your daughter could have violin lessons, her choices begin to feel like commentary on whether your sacrifice mattered. Klein would say you can't tolerate the fear that she may thrive while choosing differently from you, so you project that fear onto her as concern about her decisions. Your judgment is not really about her boyfriend's shirt or her career path. It is about managing your own fear that everything you provided may not have been necessary, that she could flourish without the standards you believed were essential. That your watchfulness was more about your need for control than her need for protection. The criticism you offer shields you from that unbearable possibility by keeping the focus on what she is doing wrong instead of examining what the habit of constant judgment costs both of you.

Asking the Question

Three weeks after Brandon's visit, Olivia called to talk about switching her graduate program from the accelerated track to the standard two-year option. Stephanie felt the familiar tightening, the early signs of a judgment forming. *That is not strategic. You will fall behind. Employers prefer the intensive program.* Her mouth opened to explain why this was a mistake, then something made her pause. The urgency to correct. The absolute certainty she knew better. The pattern she had run for decades. Instead of listing the reasons this choice was wrong, she asked an unfamiliar question. "Help me understand what you are thinking." The silence lasted long enough for Stephanie to wonder if the call had dropped. Then Olivia's voice returned different. Not defensive. Not clipped. Actually explaining. She had been burning out trying to maintain the pace while working full-time. The slower track meant she could absorb the material rather than survive it. Stephanie heard something she had missed for years. Her daughter had been making thoughtful choices all along. Stephanie just could not see them through the filter of her constant judgment.

Brené Brown's research on shame and vulnerability explains why this shift matters.[27] Her work shows that deep curiosity and judgment do not coexist in the mind; when you stay genuinely curious, the instinct to critique and defend quiets. Your brain cannot stay open and closed at the same time. The question is not a communication trick. It is an interruption that creates room for understanding instead of automatic reaction. Brown found that people who ask questions and stay in "learner" mode before offering opinions build levels of trust that people who lead with correction rarely reach. The question signals interest in another person's thinking rather than waiting for your turn to redirect it. Stephanie began practicing in smaller moments.

When a colleague approached a project differently, she asked what constraints were shaping their choices. When her sister made a parenting decision that baffled her, she grew curious about the values guiding it. Each question revealed information her judgments had been obscuring. The question "why?" can judge or wonder. Your tone decides which.

When Both Options Serve the Moment

There are moments when judgment has a place. Some situations require clarity rather than curiosity. When someone repeatedly violates a boundary, when behavior is harmful, when accountability matters more than interpretation, judgment becomes necessary. A teenager lying about their whereabouts needs consequences, not exploration. An employee missing critical deadlines needs direct feedback about performance. A friend who consistently disrespects your time needs to hear that the pattern is not acceptable. These moments call for naming what is not working. Yet they are far less common than the frequency with which most people rely on judgment would suggest. Many moments that feel like they demand critique are actually invitations for curiosity that you are treating as chances to correct.

The distinction lies in whether you are holding someone to expectations that genuinely matter or reacting to choices that simply differ from your preferences. Stephanie needed to speak directly if Olivia violated a real boundary. She did not need to scrutinize Brandon's shirt or Olivia's graduate school timeline or the hundred other decisions that did not match how she would have done things. A colleague who approaches a project differently is not violating standards. They are honoring their own way of working. Much of what becomes judgment is not about protecting anything meaningful. It is discomfort with the truth that people will make choices you would not make, and those choices may work out well anyway.

Curiosity becomes essential when you are trying to understand someone, when connection matters more than correctness, when you sense that your first interpretation might be incomplete. It becomes necessary when you notice that your judgments are creating distance you do not want. Wisdom is not choosing judgment or curiosity as fixed positions. It is learning to tell the difference between protecting something that truly needs protection and protecting your ego's need to be the authority on how life should be lived. The meta-skill is not becoming free of judgment, it's remembering that wonder and certainty can't occupy the same space.

Where This Choice Shows Up Every Day

Professional Dynamics. Your colleague handles a project in ways that seem inefficient, and you're mentally drafting feedback about the better approach. Judgment catalogs their mistakes. Curiosity asks what constraints they're working around and discovers limitations you didn't know existed. The shift from critic to collaborator means they start seeking your input instead of bracing for your corrections.

Romantic Relationships. Your partner gets emotional about something that strikes you as minor. Judgment prepares to explain why they're overreacting. Curiosity wonders what this is touching beneath the surface and asks what's really going on. They open up about feeling unsupported in ways neither of you had articulated, and the conversation goes somewhere real instead of defensive.

Family Patterns. Your adult child announces a career pivot that makes your stomach drop, and observations about financial stability queue up automatically. Judgment measures their choice against your concerns. Curiosity explores what drew them to this path. You hear values and ambitions you hadn't understood, watching someone articulate their carefully considered thinking rather than defending against your fears.

Friendship. Plans get canceled again, the third time in two months. Judgment builds a case about how little your friendship matters to them. Curiosity reaches out to understand what's actually happening and discovers a parent's declining health they haven't known how to talk about. One response ends a friendship quietly. The other offers a deepening connection.

Daily Encounters. The school volunteer makes a scheduling decision that seems baffling. Judgment drafts the email pointing out what they overlooked. Curiosity asks about the thinking behind it and learns about budget cuts and competing needs you hadn't considered. You shift from adding another complaint to helping solve the actual problem.

Practice Exercises: The Redirect

Judgment feels like clarity about someone else but it's usually information about you. These practices help you catch the certainty before it hardens into assessment, turn your attention back toward what your reaction reveals, and choose connection over being right when the relationship matters more than the correction.

Catch. When you feel judgment forming, the most powerful question is the simplest: "What if I don't actually know?" Not as a statement of ignorance, but as genuine acknowledgment that your interpretation is one perspective among many possible truths. This single question dissolves the certainty that makes judgment feel necessary. You still have observations. You just hold them more lightly.

Turn Inward. Before delivering your assessment of someone else, ask "What is my reaction teaching me about myself right now?" Your strongest judgments are often mirrors. The colleague who seems too ambitious might be reflecting your own suppressed drive. The friend who appears self-centered might be highlighting your difficulty prioritizing your needs. The parent who seems controlling might be revealing your own fears about getting it wrong. Your judgments map your internal landscape if you're willing to read them.

Perspective Shift. When someone's choice baffles you, wonder "What would make this decision make perfect sense from where they're standing?" Everyone's behavior is logical within their context, history, constraints, and values. You don't have to agree to understand. You just have to get genuinely curious about the view from their window instead of insisting they see through yours.

Invitation Test. Before offering feedback, ask "Did they actually request my input, or am I offering it because their choice makes me uncomfortable?" Real help responds to invitation. Unsolicited correction serves your anxiety, not their growth. If they didn't ask, your discomfort is information about you, not instruction for them.

Long Game. When you're about to prioritize being right, pause and ask, "What matters more to me right now, being correct or being connected?" This isn't about abandoning truth or pretending you don't have opinions. It's about recognizing that you can be absolutely right and absolutely alone. Sometimes the most loving thing you can offer isn't your wisdom. It's your willingness to not know everything while staying close anyway.

What Curiosity Creates

Eight months after that first dinner with Brandon, Stephanie sat at Thanksgiving watching Olivia and Brandon move through her kitchen with the ease of people who belonged there. The earlier version of her would have had forty observations lined up. The timing of their engagement. The financial wisdom of a wedding before Brandon finished his degree. Every observation would have been accurate. Each one would have pushed her daughter further away. Instead, when Olivia held out her hand to show the ring, Stephanie asked a question she had never thought to ask: "What excites you most about marrying him?" The conversation that followed revealed dreams Stephanie never knew her daughter held.

Olivia talked about wanting a partnership rooted in real friendship rather than shared ambition. About choosing someone who made her laugh instead of someone who looked impressive on paper. Stephanie heard her daughter naming values she had shaped intentionally, making choices with clarity, building a life that made sense even though it did not match the blueprint Stephanie had been holding. The recognition landed with unexpected force. Her daughter did not need her constant judgment to make good choices. She needed presence. She needed genuine questions. She needed Stephanie's interest in understanding her thinking instead of correcting it.

The shift showed up everywhere. At work, team members began seeking her input instead of bracing for critique because she had learned to ask what they were trying to solve before offering what she saw. Her sister called more often because their conversations no longer felt like quiet evaluations. Friendships she had strained with impossible standards began to mend. Even her relationship with herself softened. The voice that had spent decades cataloging her shortcomings quieted once she stopped practicing that habit on everyone else.

Curiosity is not weakness that overlooks everything. It is strength that prefers truth to being right. The people in your life do not need you to predict every problem or prevent every mistake. They need to feel you are genuinely interested in who they are when they are not being measured. When you choose curiosity over judgment, relationships deepen because people finally feel safe bringing their whole selves instead of only the parts they hope will pass. Your perspective becomes something people invite rather than brace against. You can keep sizing people up according to how they align with your standards, or you can discover what becomes possible when you get curious about who they actually are.

9

Lessen or Lesson

the teacher that terrifies you

The presentation slides were still glowing on Noah's laptop when he finally forced himself to look up at the conference room filled with colleagues, investors, and industry leaders who had just witnessed him unravel onstage. Three hundred people had watched him freeze for forty-seven seconds of absolute silence before stumbling through a scattered ramble that bore no resemblance to the pitch he had rehearsed for six weeks. The quarterly all-hands meeting. The moment he had been building toward for two years as Senior Product Manager. The presentation was supposed to clear the path for his promotion to Director. Instead, he delivered what could generously be called a disaster and more truthfully felt like the end of everything he had been working for.

Eight years climbing the corporate ladder through meticulous preparation and behind-the-scenes excellence, all of it dissolving in less than ten minutes of painful public collapse. Noah had always been the person who crafted the strategies, wrote the reports, designed the solutions that other people presented. He was comfortable being the mastermind behind the curtain, the one who made everyone else look good while he stayed safely in the background. But the Director role required visibility. Leadership meant standing in front of stakeholders and inspiring confidence, holding attention, answering questions in real time. It demanded exactly what he had spent his career avoiding. Being seen. Being heard. Being judged by people whose opinions shaped his future.

For six weeks he had prepared himself relentlessly. He practiced in front of mirrors, recorded himself speaking, studied executive presentation styles, memorized every transition, anticipated every question. The irony was crushing. He knew this material better than anyone in that room. He had spent two years developing the product roadmap, had run the numbers backwards and forwards, and could explain every recommendation with clarity and logic. His analysis was sound. His strategy was strong. His delivery fell apart. He started sweating visibly thirty seconds in. His voice cracked on the third word. His thoughts scattered. He lost not only his talking points but his ability to form simple sentences. The forty-seven seconds of silence while he stared at his notes felt like sinking in front of an audience he could not escape.

The shame landed heavy in his chest. Every person he had passed in the hallway after the meeting had offered sympathetic looks that felt like pity. His phone sat face-down on his desk, notifications piling up. He could not bear to look. Not yet. He could not face the concerned messages that confirmed everyone had witnessed his collapse. Now, sitting alone in his office at seven in the evening, still feeling the phantom heat of the stage lights on his skin, his mind began assembling a familiar and unforgiving story. *This is what I get for thinking I could be something I am not. I am a behind-the-scenes person. I am not leadership material. Everyone in that room knows it now. Some people are built for the spotlight. I am not one of them.*

Noah faced a choice that would determine more than his career. It would define his relationship with his own potential. He could take this failure as confirmation of every fear he carried about not being that type of person, treat the humiliation as evidence of fixed limits, decide that he was meant to support from the background while others stepped forward. Or he could ask a question that felt almost impossible. *What if this is not proof that I am unfit for leadership, but a map showing exactly what I need to learn?*

Why Your Choice Matters

Your mistakes are not proof of your limitations. They're curriculum for your development. You know the gravitational pull toward making yourself smaller after public failure. That crushing certainty that you've been exposed as inadequate, that everyone now believes you are not qualified for the role you were trying to fill. The humiliation feels like evidence of your fundamental limitations rather than temporary gaps in your skills. When you fail publicly, whether it's a presentation disaster, a relationship conflict everyone witnessed, or a creative project that falls flat, your brain's pattern recognition system goes into overdrive. The same neural networks that help you learn from experience begin working to protect you from being exposed again.

This retreat feels protective, sensible, and mature. Like finally accepting your limitations and being realistic about your capabilities. Learning your lesson about not reaching beyond your natural abilities. But psychologist Carol Dweck's research on mindset reveals a crucial distinction. People who grow from failure view their mistakes as information about what needs development rather than evidence of what they lack.[28] Her decades of research show that the difference between those who shrink after failure and those who expand is not found in natural ability or intelligence or even initial skill level. It lives in how they interpret what the failure means. A growth mindset sees setbacks as feedback about the current approach, not a fixed statement about potential. A fixed mindset sees the same setbacks as exposure of fundamental inadequacy. The truth is far simpler. Failure doesn't reveal your limits. It reveals what you haven't learned yet.

The mind that chooses to be lessened by failure asks, "What does this prove about what I can't do? How can I avoid similar exposure in the future?" These questions create a feedback loop where failure becomes evidence of inadequacy, mistakes become proof of limitations, and the logical response is to want less, try less, and risk less. But lesson consciousness asks an important question: "What if this failure isn't evidence that I don't belong here, but a roadmap for learning exactly what I need to belong here?" This single shift transforms your relationship with every mistake, every setback, and every moment that threatens to shrink you. The difference between lessen and lesson isn't about what happens to you. It's about what you do with what happens to you. When you choose lesson consciousness, you stop being a victim of your circumstances and start becoming a student of them. Three weeks after his presentation disaster, Noah's mentor asked him a question that stopped his self-recrimination cold. "What did you learn about yourself that you couldn't have learned any other way?" The question forced him to examine his failure differently. Not the outcome, but the mechanism. Not the humiliation, but the cause.

Why We Shrink After Setbacks

When you fail publicly, your sense of self absorbs a direct hit. Your mind activates protective mechanisms designed to shield your identity from information that feels incompatible with who you believe yourself to be. This is not abstract cognitive dissonance. It is physical and immediate. Your chest tightens. Your face flushes. That sick feeling in your stomach spreads through your body as shame moves through your system. Confirmation bias takes over, pulling the failure into orbit around every fear you already carry about your adequacy. Psychologist Rick Hanson's research on the brain's negativity bias explains why painful moments imprint so deeply.[29] Negative experiences cling with intensity while positive ones fade quickly, creating an internal record that overrepresents threat and underrepresents resilience.

In moments of collapse, this bias intensifies. Your brain does not isolate the current setback. It links it to every past hurt, disappointment, and loss. A single failure becomes a pattern. This always happens to me. I cannot handle pressure. I am not leadership material. And the culture we live in compounds the distortion. Optimization culture promises that with enough systems, strategies, and discipline, failure can be engineered out of existence. When you stumble, it feels like evidence that you have not optimized enough. Social platforms amplify the illusion. You see polished outcomes without the messy drafts, the missteps, or the long stretches where someone else also felt lost. You compare your lived process to someone else's curated result, and the gap feels like personal deficiency instead of the normal rhythm of growth.

The most deceptive aspect of shrinking after failure is how reasonable it feels. Pulling back from challenges feels like wisdom. Avoiding similar risks feels like learning from experience. Accepting a smaller role feels like humility. But cognitive psychology shows something different. People who interpret failures as information rather than identity develop failure resilience, the ability to recover more quickly because they stay focused on skill development instead of self-protection. Noah's turning point began when he shifted the question. Instead of asking "Why did I fail?" he asked, "What specifically went wrong, and what can I do differently next time?" That single pivot redirected his attention from self-judgment to learning.

Mining the Lesson

Three months after his presentation disaster, Noah had identified the mechanics of his failure with striking clarity. The issue was not a lack of knowledge or capability. It was that he had tried to perform confidence instead of speaking from genuine expertise. He had memorized a script that sounded impressive rather than articulating what he actually understood. When his mind went blank under pressure, he had no real foundation to fall back on. The performance unraveled because nothing underneath it felt true. No connection to his actual skill. No trust in his own grasp of the material. No authentic voice to lean on when the memorized words disappeared. This insight changed everything about how he prepared for his next opportunity.

Research by Richard Tedeschi, a psychologist who co-developed the theory of post-traumatic growth, has shown that people often develop capabilities after significant setbacks that they would not have accessed otherwise.[30] The key factor is not the severity of the setback. It is whether someone can extract specific, workable lessons from what they experienced. Tedeschi found that people who grow through difficulty share a common habit. They examine their experiences with curiosity rather than judgment. They ask what can be learned instead of what the failure says about them. This distinction often separates the setbacks that diminish from the ones that develop.

Noah's reflection revealed several concrete areas for growth. He realized he needed smaller, lower-stakes opportunities to practice public speaking, places where familiarity could gradually replace fear. He began to understand that authentic confidence would have to feel different for him. He also recognized that growth would not happen in isolation, and that he needed people who could offer honest feedback on both his content and delivery.

Each of these lessons was specific, learnable, and within reach. None of them proved he was not leadership material. Together, they outlined what leadership would require him to develop. Instead of the presentation collapse confirming his fears, it became a clear map of the skills he needed next.
The moment that could have ended his trajectory became the beginning of building genuine leadership capacity. Six months later, Noah volunteered to present quarterly updates to the executive team. Not because he had mastered public speaking, but because he had learned to speak from what he knew rather than performing what he believed leadership was supposed to look like. This is not just about recovering from failure. It is about letting difficulty become a catalyst for development rather than a reason to retreat.

When Both Options Serve the Moment

Some moments genuinely require you to step back before you can step forward. In the immediate aftermath of a painful failure, your system needs space to settle before your mind can make sense of what happened. Trying to harvest insights from an experience that still hurts is not growth. It is another kind of pressure disguised as progress. Sometimes the most important thing you can do is let yourself feel the disappointment, anger, or grief without demanding that it become useful right away.

Your body knows the difference between a pause that restores and a pause that retreats. The question is whether you can listen closely enough to tell which one you are choosing.

Temporary retreat helps when you need distance to process strong emotion, when pushing ahead would compound the strain, and when clarity is impossible because your internal world is still unsettled. This kind of intentional step back creates the breathing room needed to regain steadiness before looking more closely at what went wrong. It becomes discernment when you use it to return to yourself rather than avoid future risk. But the same step back becomes self-limiting when it shifts from protection to identity. When you begin organizing your life around avoiding situations where failure is possible. When you keep using a setback from years ago as proof that you should never try something similar again. What could have restored you instead becomes the pattern that confines you.

Growth begins when you can examine what happened with curiosity rather than criticism. When you can tell the difference between what the failure reveals about your current skills and what it says nothing about. When the emotional intensity has softened enough that you can identify specific areas for development instead of global judgments about who you are. The meta-skill is not avoiding devastation or rushing to extract meaning. It's learning to let failure change you in the ways that help you grow rather than in the ways that make you disappear.

Where This Choice Shows Up Every Day

Professional Setbacks. You miss a major deadline, lose an important account, or receive difficult feedback. Lessen tells you to stop aiming high and accept that advancement is not for you. Lesson shows you the specific skills in time management, communication, or technical execution that need refinement. The moment can either slow your growth or become the foundation for real capability.

Creative Expressions. Your presentation falls flat, your article lands quietly, your performance misses the mark. Lessen declares you lack talent and should stay where the stakes are low. Lesson highlights what needs development in audience awareness, technical skill, or authentic voice. The choice you make next determines whether this failure silences you or strengthens your craft.

Relationship Conflicts. A friendship ends painfully or a romantic relationship unravels. Lessen insists you are not good at relationships and encourages you to stay guarded. Lesson brings attention to patterns in communication, boundaries, emotional regulation, or compatibility that can help you build healthier connections. The experience stops being proof of inadequacy when you begin asking what it can teach you about creating something better.

Learning New Skills. You struggle with a language, instrument, sport, or technical ability more than you expected. Lessen whispers that you lack natural talent and should step back before anyone notices. Lesson uncovers the learning strategies, practice rhythms, and mindset shifts that support growth. Struggle becomes a map for how you learn rather than a verdict on what you cannot do.

Leadership Opportunities. You make mistakes managing a team, organizing an event, or leading a project that matters. Lessen convinces you that leadership is not your strength and that you belong in the background. Lesson teaches you about delegation, communication under pressure, and grounded authority. Those missteps become the place where leadership capacity begins rather than the place where it ends.

Practice Exercises: The Courage Debrief

Setbacks carry both shame and information, but only one moves you forward. These practices help you separate what happened from what it means about you, identify what can actually be developed, and recognize whether the moment is asking you to retreat or grow.

Shame Separation Process. When facing a significant setback, begin by separating the feeling of shame from the information contained in what happened. Shame speaks in judgments about who you are. The information describes what actually occurred. Allow yourself to feel disappointment about the outcome without letting it define your potential. Notice where shame shows up in your body. The heat in your face. The weight in your chest. The tightness in your throat. Acknowledge these sensations without allowing them to determine the meaning of the experience.

Skill Gap Analysis. Instead of asking, "Why did this happen to me?" shift the question to "What capabilities would have made a different outcome more likely?" This moves attention away from character judgment and toward development. Write down three skills that could realistically be learned or strengthened. Avoid broad traits like being more confident. Stay with concrete capabilities, such as practicing speaking without notes or developing clearer opening hooks that hold attention.

Authenticity Exploration. Consider whether the disappointing result came from trying to perform as someone you are not rather than developing who you actually are. Ask whether you were expressing your genuine abilities or attempting to inhabit a role you believed was required. Disappointing outcomes often reveal the distance between performed confidence and lived competence. Notice what might shift if you approached the challenge as yourself rather than as who you thought you should be.

Growth Edge Recognition. Notice that meaningful setbacks often occur when you are reaching beyond what is familiar. Rather than treating difficulty as a signal to retreat, consider it as information about where your growth edge may be. Comfort rarely produces change. Discomfort often marks the place where development begins.

Two-Question Investigation. After the initial impact has settled, return to the experience with two questions: How is this moment inviting contraction? How is it inviting expansion? Notice which question feels easier to answer and which feels more resistant. The question that resists you often points toward what is asking to be developed.

What Your Hardest Teacher Reveals

Two years after his presentation disaster, Noah was invited to speak at an industry conference on product innovation. The same person who once froze in front of 300 colleagues was now sharing his insights with 1,500 professionals. Something fundamental had changed. He was no longer trying to prove he belonged on the stage. He was not performing confidence or hiding behind memorized lines. He was offering what he actually knew, hoping it might help someone else avoid the mistakes he had made and use the lessons he had learned. The talk was not perfect. He still felt nervous. His voice still shook at the start. But it was useful. Authentic expertise, shared honestly, creates far more value than polished performance ever will.

Every time you choose lesson over lessen, you are practicing a different relationship with your own development. You are teaching yourself that mistakes offer information rather than verdicts, that setbacks reveal growth edges rather than permanent limits, and that difficulty can shape you without diminishing you. This practice builds slowly. The first few times feel vulnerable and unsettling because you are looking directly at what you would rather avoid. But each time you pull learning from an experience that once would have shrunk you, you build a steadier kind of confidence. Not the fragile confidence that depends on avoiding failure, but the durable confidence that comes from knowing you can grow through anything.

The opposite path unfolds quietly. You begin declining opportunities that carry real risk. You choose projects where success feels guaranteed instead of challenges that could stretch your abilities. Your world contracts until you are living inside a smaller version of yourself, one curated to protect your sense of adequacy rather than expand it. What once felt like safety becomes confinement. The routines that once steadied you begin to limit you. The protection you built becomes the boundary you cannot move beyond, not because you lack potential, but because you stopped stepping toward it.

Your mistakes do not define your limits. They reveal your learning edges, the exact places where you are invited to grow beyond who you have been into who you are capable of becoming. Your willingness to be imperfect in service of becoming skilled becomes the foundation for every capability you will build, every relationship you will strengthen, and every moment when you discover that your real self is far more capable than your performed self ever was. Each setback carries information. Each difficulty contains instruction. Every hard moment can become fuel for your development.

10

Perfect or Progress

the fantasy that steals your reality

Alex's hands were shaking, but not from the cold. He stood in the Icelandic darkness at 11:43 p.m., forty-four kilometers outside Reykjavik, surrounded by two dozen photographers whose tripods formed a semicircle facing north. The sky had begun its performance twenty minutes earlier, ribbons of green and violet unfolding exactly as he had imagined for five years. Exactly as he had studied in tutorials, articles, and forums. But his camera would not focus. His gloves were rated for Arctic temperatures, but the cold still seeped through as he pressed buttons he had memorized in theory but never practiced in real conditions. He adjusted settings he could explain with confidence yet had never tested, not once, in actual darkness. The viewfinder showed nothing but blur while around him, shutters clicked steadily, capturing the show he had traveled thousands of miles to photograph.

"First time shooting the aurora?" The woman beside him did not look up from her camera, her hands moving with the ease of someone who had learned through doing. "Yeah," Alex said, which was technically true, but not honest. This wasn't just his first time shooting the aurora. It was his first time shooting anything. Fourteen months earlier he had bought top-tier equipment. A mirrorless body, three premium lenses, a professional tripod. He had unboxed everything with reverence, read the manual cover to cover, watched every tutorial he could find. Then he had repacked it all carefully, waiting for the moment when he would be good enough to deserve using it.

Except that moment never came, because he had confused studying with practicing. He knew ISO, aperture, and shutter speed the way you know choreography from watching instead of dancing. He could explain long-exposure techniques with precision but was still unable to execute them. The aurora brightened, pillars of light rising across the horizon, and the photographers around him adjusted their settings with practiced ease. Alex's screen showed only darkness and blur. His months of preparation, the meticulous research, the careful planning had equipped him for perfection, but not for reality.

He had been preparing endlessly while refusing to attempt anything he could not execute flawlessly. He had imagined becoming a photographer without ever being willing to take imperfect photographs. "Here," the woman said gently, reaching for his camera. "Let me see your settings." The kindness made his throat tighten. She could fix his exposure in seconds. But that would mean acknowledging what he had been avoiding. He had called himself a photographer for more than a year, talked about launching a portfolio, posted inspiration instead of work. Yet he had avoided the one thing that mattered most. Being willing to be a beginner.

The aurora peaked, filling the sky with moving color. This was the moment he had built everything around. And he was standing there watching other people capture it while his equipment sat useless in his hands. Alex faced the choice he had avoided since the day he bought the camera. He could hand it to a stranger and admit he had been preparing without practicing. Or he could cling to the illusion that he would try again someday, once he was finally good enough to begin.

Standing in the cold, surrounded by the evidence of his perfect preparation and complete inexperience, Alex saw something with startling clarity. His problem wasn't that he lacked talent. It was that he had demanded mastery before allowing himself a first attempt. Perfect progress had kept him motionless. The only way forward required the thing he feared most. Taking an imperfect first shot.

Why Your Choice Matters

The most seductive lie you tell yourself sounds like wisdom. *I'll start when I'm ready.* The pattern becomes so familiar you barely notice it. The goal you will pursue when you have more time. The skill you will develop when you can afford better equipment. The conversation you will have when you find the perfect words. The project you will begin once you feel fully prepared. Someday arrives disguised as prudence. It seems responsible. It seems mature. It feels like prudence, as if careful people wait for the right moment because important things deserve proper preparation.

Perfect preparation is procrastination disguised as progress. The someday mindset treats your current self as a draft and your future self as a polished version who will finally live the life you imagine. Psychologists call this temporal displacement, the tendency to push meaningful action into an imagined future where conditions are ideal and your abilities somehow expand to match your hopes. But future you is not better equipped to begin. Future you is simply more practiced at waiting. Research shows something we would rather ignore. Future you will face the same fears, constraints, and hesitations as current you, along with the added weight of delay.

Choosing progress over perfect preparation shifts you from imagining future action to creating something real through present effort. You stop waiting for ideal conditions and allow yourself to begin imperfectly. This is not abandoning planning or acting carelessly. It's recognizing that planning can become a substitute for action, research can turn into avoidance, and the perfect moment to begin is the myth that keeps you from discovering what you can do. Studies on learning show that people who begin before they feel ready and improve through iteration consistently outperform those who invest the same time polishing their plan before taking a first step. The difference is not talent. It is the willingness to be temporarily unskilled on the way to becoming capable.

Alex discovered this standing beneath the aurora with a camera he had never actually used. His three years of preparation had been elaborate theater, the appearance of working toward something while avoiding the vulnerability of trying it. He had studied everything except what it felt like to press the shutter and find out what he could create. Resistance to being a beginner is often the only thing standing between you and mastery.

Why We Mistake Planning for Progress

Think about the last time you told someone about a goal. Did you describe what you were doing, or what you were planning to do? The difference is subtle but significant. When you attempt something meaningful, your mind offers a tempting shortcut. Industrial-Organizational Psychologist Piers Steel's research on procrastination shows that we respond strongly to immediate rewards, which is why planning, buying equipment, and organizing can feel satisfying enough to stand in for real progress.[31] Some psychologists call this preparation pride, the sense of accomplishment that comes from getting ready rather than doing the work. Your brain reacts similarly to both. Planning feels productive even when it changes nothing.

The trap deepens as the stakes rise. The more you care and the more you want to get it right, the more elaborate your preparation becomes. It shields you from the possibility of failing at something that matters. B.J. Fogg, a behavioral scientist and founder of the Stanford Behavior Design Lab, shows through his research on behavior change that people consistently overestimate future motivation and underestimate present barriers.[32] You imagine a future version of yourself who is more disciplined, more focused, and perfectly ready. You design plans that depend on ideal circumstances and sustained enthusiasm. Then real life intervenes, and the perfect moment never arrives.

The digital world intensifies this habit. Optimization culture suggests that the right tools, systems, and preparation can spare you from the messy reality of learning through trial and error. You consume content about productivity while producing nothing. You follow creators who make their work look effortless while hiding the years of imperfect attempts behind the scenes. You can research endlessly without beginning. You can collect tutorials, courses, and inspiration boards that simulate momentum while keeping you at a distance from the discomfort of trying. Pinterest boards fill with projects you intend to do. Browser tabs multiply with articles you plan to read. Shopping carts gather gear you might use someday. All of it feels productive because you are taking action, just not the action that moves you forward. You stay busy preparing while the work itself never actually starts.

Owning Your Amateur Status

Three weeks after Iceland, Alex stood in his apartment holding the same camera, but something in him had shifted. On the flight home, instead of planning his next perfect trip, he scrolled through the handful of images he had taken after the woman beside him helped adjust his settings. They were objectively bad. Blurry. Underexposed. Unmistakably amateur. But they existed. They were real photographs, not imagined ones. That night he stepped outside and began shooting again: his neighborhood at dusk, the coffee shop he passed every morning, his own desk. He shot badly, often. But he was learning what no amount of research could have taught him. What his hands discovered while adjusting settings. What his eyes understood only through the lens, not in imagined conditions.

Neuroscientist Daniel Levitin's research on skill acquisition reveals that expertise requires thousands of hours of deliberate practice.[33] Preparation culture forgets the essential qualifier. Those hours must involve doing the thing, not thinking about doing it. Playing music badly for 10,000 hours develops musicianship. Reading about music theory for 10,000 hours develops commentary. The path to excellence runs through a long stretch of lived mediocrity. This reality terrifies anyone who cares deeply about being good at something. It means the only way to become excellent is to tolerate being unskilled, to create work that doesn't yet meet your standards, to attempt skills you have not yet mastered, and to show up as an amateur long before you can claim expertise.

Progress asks you to accept a truth that feels both simple and disruptive. You cannot perfect your way into readiness, you can only practice your way into capability. The writer must draft work that disappoints them. The speaker must stumble through early talks. The artist must make pieces that feel unfinished. The entrepreneur must launch before the product is complete. Excellence is not the absence of failure. It is what emerges after you have gathered enough imperfect attempts to understand what actually works. Your early efforts will fall short of your own taste, which was shaped by consuming the polished work of people with years of practice you have not yet lived. That gap between vision and ability is not evidence you lack talent. It is the landscape of growth itself.

When Both Options Serve the Moment

Some situations genuinely require mastery before action. Surgery demands extensive training before touching a patient. Structural engineering calls for precise calculations before the first beam is placed. Financial commitments deserve thoughtful analysis before money is at risk. The question is not whether preparation matters. It is whether the preparation you are doing builds real capability or quietly protects you from beginning. Preparation serves you when it rehearses the actual skill under real conditions, when it has a clear endpoint that leads to movement, or when it targets specific gaps rather than soothing general anxiety about starting.

Planning shifts into protection when you cycle through the same research without new understanding, when every insight becomes another reason to wait, and when polishing the plan replaces practicing the skill. This version of preparation gives you the feeling of diligence while keeping you safely distant from the vulnerability of trying. The activity looks responsible on the surface, but underneath it reinforces a belief that you must eliminate every possibility of error before taking a single step. That belief quietly drains courage. You are learning more about control than capability, and the work that would move you forward remains untouched. Honest self-examination asks a simple question: Are you preparing to act, or preparing to avoid acting?

The difference becomes clearer when you pay attention to how each option feels. Genuine unreadiness is steady and specific about what must still be learned. Fear-based avoidance is restless, urgent, and full of shifting explanations. One helps you grow. The other keeps you circling the starting line. Integration means valuing both kinds of preparation. The knowledge that builds a foundation and the courage that builds momentum. Some work requires competence before practice. Other work requires practice before clarity. The meta-skill is not lowering your standards. It's recognizing when effort expands your ability and when it only protects you from the necessary awkwardness of learning by doing.

Where This Choice Shows Up Every Day

Professional Communication. You rewrite the same email, revise your resume for weeks, or hold a portfolio you never share. Perfect keeps polishing, searching for flaws, and postponing the moment of exposure. Progress sends the solid draft, applies with the resume that reflects where you are, and shares the work that represents your current ability rather than a future ideal.

Difficult Conversations. You rehearse every line, wait for the perfect timing, and script every possible response. Perfect delays until the conditions feel flawless. Progress speaks now, accepts the stumbles that come with honesty, and trusts that real connection grows from sincerity, not precision.

Family Dynamics. You study parenting strategies, plan the ideal gathering, or wait to raise a sensitive topic until the approach feels immaculate. Perfect waits for the right method and the right moment. Progress begins the conversation with humility, hosts the good-enough gathering, and steps into difficult topics even without a perfect plan.

Career Development. You purchase courses you never complete, research career changes endlessly, or collect equipment for hobbies you never practice. Perfect mistakes preparation for movement and acquisition for mastery. Progress practices the skill badly for fifteen minutes today, submits the good-enough application, or walks into the beginner class without needing to look talented.

Health and Habits. You design ideal workout routines, research nutrition endlessly, or wait for motivation that never arrives. Perfect waits for flawless conditions. Progress takes the short walk, does the imperfect workout, chooses one better meal, and starts the habit now instead of waiting for the version of you who feels ready.

Practice Exercises: The Good Enough Audit

Perfectionism promises excellence but delivers delay. These practices help you define what good enough actually looks like, release work before it feels ready, and discover that progress happens through imperfect action rather than flawless preparation.

The 80% Rule. Before you begin, define what good enough actually means. Identify the minimum viable version that delivers value rather than the perfect version you imagine. Set that as the finish line for your first attempt. You can revise something that exists. You cannot revise something that is still waiting for a flawless beginning.

The Done Date. Give every project a completion date that arrives sooner than you would prefer. Commit to releasing whatever exists on that day. Not the version you hoped you would have. The version you actually have. This forces clarity about what matters and prevents perfectionism from consuming all your time with work that looks productive while changing very little.

The 15-Minute Proof. Choose one goal you have been preparing for and spend fifteen minutes today doing it. Not planning or researching. Doing. Set a timer. When it ends, you can stop. But you must begin. Notice what becomes clear only through action, the kind of learning preparation could never produce.

The Perfectionism Reality Check. When you find yourself polishing endlessly, pause and ask three questions: Am I meaningfully improving this or simply altering it? What would happen if I sent or shared this today? What opportunity am I avoiding by continuing to perfect it? These questions reveal whether you are serving the work or serving your anxiety.

The Imperfect Record. Create a record of moments when your unfinished, imperfect efforts moved you forward anyway. Note the projects that succeeded despite early flaws, the feedback that improved your work after release, the learning that came only through mistakes. Over time you will see a pattern. Progress rarely begins with mastery. It begins with willingness.

The Reality Found in Beginning

Six months after Iceland, Alex had built a portfolio of aurora photographs that was far from perfect but unmistakably his. He had returned twice more, each trip teaching him what no book or video ever could. His images began appearing in travel magazines, not because they were technically flawless but because they were alive. Each frame carried the perspective of someone who had shown up fully, imperfect but present. More importantly, Alex no longer described himself as someone who hoped to become a photographer. He *was* one. He still deleted most of what he shot. He still produced work that disappointed him. But his photographs existed in the world instead of remaining trapped in the safety of his own imagination. The three years he spent preparing had not made him a photographer. Three months of taking imperfect shots had.

Excellence asks for thousands of hours of mediocrity first, not as punishment but as the path itself. When you choose progress over perfect preparation, you step out of the illusion that keeps your best work waiting for a future version of you. This choice determines whether your dreams stay imagined or become lived, whether your abilities grow through use or slowly fade through protection. The cost of perfectionism is not only delayed action. It is the loss of creating for its own sake, the satisfaction of finishing something, the humility that comes from feedback, and the quiet pride of bringing something real into the world. You cannot refine what does not yet exist. No amount of preparation can substitute for the learning that only comes through doing.

Success has never been about flawlessness. It is about staying devoted to something larger than your ego's need to appear competent. You become someone who learns faster because you risk feedback sooner. Someone who creates more because you act more often. Someone who contributes more because you choose truth over polish. Your willingness to begin before you feel ready becomes the foundation for every capability you will develop, every project you will finish, and the life you will shape through imperfect momentum. You do not need the perfect moment. You need the courage to begin while uncertainty remains. Everything else unfolds once you are in motion.

11

Perform or Reveal

the mask that everyone believes

Ben sat in his home office at 6:23 a.m. rehearsing for the nine o'clock executive presentation, practicing the voice he had been performing for twenty-two years. Not *his* voice. The voice he learned after watching which executives rose and which were quietly managed out. Assertive but not aggressive. Data-driven but warm. Strategic but approachable. A voice that sounded nothing like him, yet everyone at work believed it was who he was. His phone buzzed with a text from Jim, his college roommate who had just opened a custom furniture shop in the mountains. "Dude, remember when we said we'd do this together? I need a partner. Real offer. Think about it." Ben set the phone down and returned to his notes on operational efficiency and strategic realignment. Words that meant nothing to him but everything to the people who would decide his future.

The presentation went perfectly because Ben had learned exactly how to be perfect in rooms like this. Every line landed. Every transition flowed. He made eye contact at the right moments, laughed at the CEO's jokes, pivoted smoothly when questioned. Afterward, three colleagues congratulated him. "You're so natural up there," one said, and something in Ben's chest tightened. Natural. Twenty-two years of calculated performance mistaken for authenticity. At lunch his boss mentioned they were considering him for Senior Vice President. Ben's stomach dropped instead of lifting. The promotion would mean more money, more respect, and more years showing up as Corporate Ben while the person he might have been receded even further.

That evening he escaped to the garage where a rocking chair sat half-finished, cedar and walnut joined with a precision that required his full attention. Out here his hands knew what to do. No script. No persona. Just wood, tools, and the quiet satisfaction of making something that would last. His daughter, Eleanor, appeared in the doorway and ran her hand along the curved armrest. "Dad, this is beautiful. You could actually sell this. Why don't you?" The question landed somewhere he had avoided for years. Ben looked at the chair and felt the distance between who he was in this garage and who he pretended to be everywhere else.

Later that night he stood in the workshop at 10:15 holding two futures in his hands. Jim's text offered partnership in a small shop building furniture for people who cared about craftsmanship. Real work creating real things that mattered. The SVP path offered $80,000 more, a better title, and deeper respect from people who knew Corporate Ben but had never met the person underneath. It promised more years perfecting a role he had never wanted while telling himself this was what responsible adults did. You didn't upend your life at forty-six because you liked building furniture on weekends. You didn't walk away from security, the kind twenty-two years of disciplined saving and sound investment had built, because something inside you felt hollow.

He thought about Eleanor starting high school. His son Jack's extracurricular activity expenses. The mortgage. Andrea's parents who bragged about their son-in-law the VP. He thought about being seventy and looking back at a life spent becoming exceptionally good at being someone he wasn't. The wood shavings on his workshop floor felt more honest than anything in his corner office. But honesty meant disappointing the people who believed in the version of him he had built over decades. It meant admitting he had constructed a role and mistaken it for himself. The choice was not about a promotion or a business. It was about whether he would continue performing until the performance was all that remained, or finally risk letting someone see who he had been hiding all along.

Why Your Choice Matters

You spend years constructing a version of yourself that earns respect, and somewhere along the way that constructed version begins to feel like the only one you have. The careful shaping starts innocently. You notice which behaviors get rewarded and which get dismissed. You learn what earns seriousness and what invites ridicule. You adjust. You adapt. You amplify the parts of you that work and quiet the parts that don't. It feels like growth, like becoming more professional or more mature. But something subtler happens beneath the polish. You don't just learn strategic presentation. You learn to disappear behind it.

Donald Winnicott, a British psychoanalyst, spent decades describing how people develop what he called the false self, an adaptive facade that forms when expressing the spontaneous, real self feels unsafe or unwelcome.[34] He found that children who learned early that their true feelings or preferences weren't acceptable began constructing versions of themselves designed to secure approval. The false self is not deliberate deception. It's adaptation that becomes automatic. What begins as a way to fit in gradually becomes the default way you exist in the world. Over time the performance becomes so seamless you no longer notice the distance between who you are and who you learned to be. You wake up one day and realize the version that once felt temporary has become the only one everyone knows.

Perform operates with persuasive logic. If you can become polished enough, impressive enough, and successful enough as the constructed version, you will finally feel secure. If you master the presentation, the approval it earns will make the effort worthwhile. But the mechanism traps you in place. The better you get at performing, the more you are rewarded for staying in character. Every compliment, every promotion, every comment about how natural you seem reinforces the identity you crafted rather than the one you abandoned. You are not simply chasing success. You are maintaining a persona that depends on continuous performance, and the praise that comes with it makes stopping feel impossible.

Reveal asks a question that feels disorienting. What if the approval you are chasing only matters because you stopped approving of the person underneath? What if the identity you have perfected is the very thing keeping you from feeling alive? The version you have been maintaining is not your fullest potential. It is your authenticity quietly replaced by adaptation. Somewhere between learning how to be taken seriously and becoming someone others admire, you stopped asking whether you admire the version you have become. The performance that protected you at twenty-four constrains you at forty-six. You became so practiced at being someone else that you forgot being yourself was available to you all along.

Why We Build the Wrong Self

The performance you have been maintaining did not begin with career ambitions or professional strategy. It began the first time you learned that some parts of you were welcomed and other parts were not. Maybe your parents praised your responsibility but dismissed you when you were playful. Maybe teachers rewarded compliance and punished creativity. Maybe peers accepted the edited version of you but withdrew when you showed anything raw or uncertain. You learned to reveal what drew approval and hide what did not, and that lesson became the foundation for everything that followed. The performance was not manipulation, it was survival shaped as adaptation. You were not choosing to be inauthentic. You were choosing the version of yourself that felt safest to reveal.

James Masterson, a prominent American psychiatrist, spent his career exploring how people develop a defensive self-presentation, a more rigid pattern in which the authentic self is gradually set aside in favor of a compliant identity designed to secure attachment and approval.[35] He found that children who received conditional love, acceptance tied to specific behaviors or achievements rather than their inherent worth, learned that belonging required performance. The real self with its messy feelings and inconvenient desires began to feel risky. The performed self that pleased others became essential. What you experienced as growing up was often a careful pruning of whatever did not fit the acceptable mold. By adulthood, the performance became so practiced that distinguishing it from personality felt almost impossible.

This pattern intensifies in environments that reward presentation over substance. Corporate cultures that promote people who look the part. Social circles that value image more than honesty. Families that prioritize appearances over emotional truth. You learned to read rooms quickly, adjusting yourself with the precision of someone who understood the stakes. The adaptation felt intelligent because it worked. You were promoted. Included. Praised. Each success reinforced the belief that the performed version was necessary, and that whatever lived underneath was not enough to carry you forward.

The cost does not surface all at once. It appears quietly in moments that should feel like victories. The promotion that leaves you feeling strangely hollow. The compliment about being natural that tightens something in your chest. The family dinner where your spouse and children interact with the polished version of you because that is the version that is present everywhere now. You are not invisible or unknown. You are celebrated and connected to people who have never met the version of you that lives beneath the performance. The adaptation worked so well that loosening it feels destabilizing. After so many years embodying the constructed version, revealing anything more authentic feels less like honesty and more like stepping into unfamiliar territory you are not sure anyone asked to see.

Dropping the Script

Revealing does not require dramatic confession or the dismantling of your entire life. It begins with small acts of authenticity in moments where performance feels automatic. Ben's shift did not begin when he considered leaving his job. It began when he called Jim back and admitted he was uncertain instead of manufacturing confidence. The conversation felt more honest than years of polished presentations because he was not trying to sound like someone who had it figured out. He allowed himself to be someone who did not. The revelation was not in what he said. It was in what he stopped performing. The script he had followed for two decades, the careful calibration of tone and posture and certainty, loosened when he spoke from genuine curiosity rather than strategic positioning.

That unguarded honesty felt terrifying and necessary at the same time.

Authenticity develops through practice in moments that feel manageable before extending to moments that carry more risk. You do not dismantle an entire performance at once. You start by letting the mask slip where the stakes feel lower. Admitting to a colleague that you are still working out a solution instead of reaching for corporate language. Telling your partner something true about what feels difficult rather than offering the polished explanation that protects your image. Allowing your children to see you uncertain or imperfect instead of maintaining the illusion of complete control. These small experiments test the catastrophe you have spent years anticipating. What you usually discover is that people respond to authenticity with relief rather than the rejection you feared.

The mechanism works through accumulated evidence that challenges the belief system that built the performance in the first place. Each time you reveal something real and remain intact, you confront the assumption that your authentic self is unacceptable. The colleague does not judge your uncertainty. They collaborate more openly. Your partner does not lose respect, they feel closer to someone who is actually present. Your children do not see weakness, they see a parent who is human. Slowly, you learn that the version of you that lives underneath the performance creates more genuine connection than the version you perfected to avoid risk. The constructed self promised safety. The authentic self offers belonging.

When Both Options Serve the Moment

Not every moment calls for full transparency. A job interview is not the place to catalog your doubts about being qualified. A client presentation is not where you disclose your imposter syndrome. A child asking if everything will be okay during a divorce does not need the full weight of your fear. Erving Goffman, a sociologist who pioneered a "dramaturgical" view of social life, observed that people move through life wearing different roles, adjusting their presentation depending on what the moment requires.[36] This flexibility is not deception. It is part of how humans navigate complex social worlds. The line between healthy and harmful performing lives in what happens when the moment ends. Healthy performing has an off switch. You show up polished for the pitch, then return to yourself when you walk through the door. The role serves a purpose, then releases you.

Toxic performing has no off switch. The professional voice follows you to dinner. The curated version dominates every conversation. You perform competence with your partner, perform calm with your children, perform success with friends until the role feels more familiar than the person underneath it. This does not happen suddenly. It happens through repetition. You adapt in one setting, then carry the adaptation into another, until the performed version becomes the one everyone expects and the one you no longer remember how to remove. Some situations truly require the role. An employee in crisis needs steadiness more than your confusion. An aging parent facing a health scare needs reassurance more than your unfiltered fear. These moments call for temporary restraint, not permanent concealment.

Discernment lives in whether you have places where the performance stops. Friends who hear the unedited version of your thoughts. A partner who knows what you are actually wrestling with. Quiet hours where you are not managing anyone's perception, including your own. When performing protects someone else during genuine difficulty, you are offering care. When performing protects you from being seen, you are choosing distance. Adaptation can be a skill that strengthens connection when used wisely. It becomes self-abandonment only when it replaces who you are rather than expressing a temporary role. The meta-skill is choosing authenticity as your foundation, while knowing when brief departures serve the moment instead of becoming the way you live.

Where This Choice Shows Up Every Day

Professional Settings. Your boss asks how you are managing the new workload and you automatically say you are fine while quietly falling behind. Perform maintains the appearance of competence even as burnout builds. Reveal says you are stretched thin and need to revisit priorities. The honesty creates space for real solutions instead of silent collapse.

Personal Relationships. Your partner asks what is wrong and you default to reassurance because admitting struggle feels like weakness. Perform protects the image of having everything under control. Reveal shares that you have been anxious about work and taking it out on them without meaning to. The truth deepens connection rather than creating distance through forced ease.

Parenting. Your teenager asks if you ever feel lost and you reach for certainty you do not actually feel. Perform projects confidence to protect them from your uncertainty. Reveal offers that sometimes you do feel unsure and that being an adult does not mean having all the answers. The authenticity teaches them that uncertainty is human, not failure.

Friendship. You post carefully curated moments that show only success, celebration, and ease while scrolling through your feed feeling increasingly disconnected from your own life. Perform crafts the highlight reel that maintains the image of having it together. Reveal shares the messy middle with someone who matters, admitting the promotion came with panic attacks or the vacation photo hid an argument. The honesty transforms performance anxiety into actual friendship.

Family Dynamics. You arrive at family gatherings as the successful version they expect even when your actual life feels unsteady. Perform maintains the image that keeps questions away. Reveal allows others to see you as you are rather than who you think you need to be. The honesty invites a kind of support that performance can never access.

Practice Exercises: The Authenticity Pilot

Performance becomes invisible when you've been doing it long enough. These practices help you notice when you're shaping yourself for an audience, recognize the cost of constant curation, and experiment with what happens when you stop managing how you're perceived.

The Two Voice Detection. For one day, pay close attention to how you speak in meetings and meaningful conversations. Mentally tag your statements as either *P* for the performance voice or *R* for the reveal voice. Performance sounds polished, strategic, or image-protecting. Reveal sounds grounded, imperfect, and true. Do not change anything yet. Simply observe. You may discover you have been performing so automatically that you no longer recognize your real voice when it appears. Awareness always precedes change. You cannot remove a mask you don't realize you are wearing.

The Micro Truth Injection. Once a day, add a single sentence of truth you would normally edit out. Not confession. Not crisis. Just something real. Perhaps you say that today has been harder than you expected or that you are still sorting out how you feel. These small expressions train your nervous system to tolerate authenticity in manageable doses. You learn that people respond with understanding rather than the rejection your performance was designed to prevent.

The Un-Editing Pass. Choose one email or message you wrote today. Highlight every sentence you adjusted to sound more impressive, agreeable, or strategic. Beneath each, write the unedited version, the one you would use if your only goal was clarity rather than image. The distance between the two versions reveals how much of your communication serves performance rather than connection.

The Shadow Role Interview. Treat your performed self as if it were a role you hired long ago. Ask it simple questions: What is your purpose? What threat are you protecting me from? Whose approval are you working for? What cost do you create when you take over? These answers expose the logic behind the false self, the fears it was built to manage, and the moments when it steps in without being asked.

The Stranger Test. Choose a low-stakes environment where no one knows you and practice showing up without performance behaviors for one hour. A coffee shop. A gym class. A community event. No strategic framing. No curated tone. No managing perception. Notice what becomes easier when you stop shaping yourself around imagined expectations. This helps you rediscover the baseline version of you, the one that exists when performance has no function to serve.

What Was Always Possible

Six months after the phone call with Jim, Ben stood in their workshop watching sunlight move through sawdust while a client described what she needed in a dining table. Not the strategic listening he had perfected in conference rooms, where every word was weighed for positioning. Just simple curiosity about how a family of five used their space. He had taken the partnership, given notice at the pharmaceutical company, and stepped off the SVP track that would have locked him into another decade of performing competence he no longer believed in. Driving away from that office felt less like loss and more like being able to breathe again.

The hardest part was not the pay cut or the uncertainty. It was realizing how many relationships had been built around the performed version of him. Colleagues who stopped calling once he was no longer useful to their networks. Friends who had connected with Corporate Ben but had little interest in the person building furniture. His father asked twice if he was having a midlife crisis, unable to understand why anyone would walk away from the status he had spent decades earning. Some connections faded. Others deepened in ways Ben had not expected. Eleanor began showing him her artwork again, something she had stopped doing when his responses turned into performative praise. Jack asked him to help coach soccer. Andrea said it felt like being married to someone who was actually present, rather than someone constantly rehearsing for the next performance.

What surprised Ben most was the energy he had been spending maintaining the performance: the effort required to track which version of himself each person expected, to monitor every word for strategic effect, to keep the competent facade from cracking. Without that constant management, he slept better and laughed more. He was present in conversations instead of calculating responses. The work that had once been refuge from performance became simply his work. He no longer needed refuge because he was no longer hiding. After the client left a deposit, Jim walked over and gestured toward the stack of custom orders. He looked at Ben and said, "You smile different now. Less like you should and more like you mean it."

Ben looked at his hands, still adjusting to the calluses that came from creating something real instead of performing someone else's expectations. Twenty-two years constructing a version of himself that looked successful while the real version waited for permission to exist. Every time you choose to reveal instead of perform, you teach yourself that being seen is more sustaining than being admired, that authentic connection lasts longer than polished impression, that the energy used to maintain performance could build the life you have been trying to imitate. Your relationships deepen because people meet the person beneath the facade. Your work becomes yours instead of a role you were taught to play. You can keep exhausting yourself to maintain the performance everyone believes in, or you can let them see the person you have been all along.

12

Presence or Distraction

the here that keeps disappearing

Eli set his folding chair on the sideline the same way he did every Saturday morning, angled toward the field with a coffee in one hand and the illusion of presence in the other. He told people he loved showing up for his daughter, and he meant it, but never fully inhabited it. He arrived early, helped carry the team cooler from another parent's SUV, and made small comments about the tournament next weekend. But the moment the whistle blew, a different rhythm took over, the rhythm that governed most of his life. The phone vibrated once, then again, then again. Slack messages. WhatsApp threads. Emails. Reminders. Each notification tugging at him until his attention slid off the field without him noticing it happen.

By the third minute of the game he was answering a supplier crisis. By the seventh he was drafting a message to a potential investor. By the tenth he had stepped away from the sideline to take a call because the wind made the audio hard to hear. His daughter, Ivy, scanned the sideline the way she always did, searching for his face at a particular moment in the play. Instead she saw the empty chair and turned back to the field without showing any visible disappointment. This was their pattern. At dinner, Eli took calls between bites. At Target, he paused the cart to respond to messages. At restaurants, he stepped outside so often that servers learned to wait before delivering entrees. At bedtime, Ivy spoke into the space where his attention should have been, waiting for his eyes to lift from the screen long enough to meet hers.

When Eli returned to the sideline after twelve minutes outside the fence, he sat with intention. Today would be different. He would stay fully present, watch every remaining moment, give Ivy the attention she deserved. But each time his phone lit up, his eyes dropped before he realized it was happening. Just a quick check. Nothing important would happen in the next few seconds. A glance became a scroll. A scroll became a reply. A reply became a paragraph he did not remember beginning. Presence was not a moment. It was a muscle he had never strengthened. Distraction was the reflex that felt as natural as breathing. By halftime, Ivy had blocked two shots, made one assist, and stolen the ball three times. Eli saw none of it.

During the team huddle, Eli called out encouragement and offered Ivy a thumbs up when she caught his eye. She nodded, polite and self-contained, something in her expression held too still. After the huddle broke, she jogged back onto the field without looking over again. The second half opened with a burst of energy. Parents cheering. Girls sprinting. Coaches shouting reminders. Eli's phone vibrated once more. He told himself he would not answer. It could wait. But the vibration struck the part of him that confused urgency with importance and he tapped the screen before he knew he had done it. While he typed, Ivy made a play so beautiful the entire sideline gasped. She intercepted a pass, weaved between two defenders, and sent the ball into the upper corner of the net. The crowd erupted. Coaches raised their arms. Teammates swarmed her.

Eli looked up halfway through the celebration and realized he had missed not only the goal but the moment Ivy turned toward the sideline looking for him. Her eyes had already moved on. The rest of the game passed in a blur he pretended to watch. When the final whistle blew and parents folded their chairs, Ivy walked to the car ahead of him without waiting. She did not say anything. She didn't need to. He felt something shift between them, a widening he could no longer explain away. Not distance created by absence, but distance created by a presence offered in pieces too small to matter. For the first time, Eli wondered if distraction was not something happening to him but something he kept choosing without noticing, shaping his life into a collection of moments he always assumed he could catch later. Except later always looked the same.

Why Your Choice Matters

You tell yourself you are still here. Close enough to hear the crowd. Close enough to catch the highlights. Close enough that it feels unfair to call it absence. But distraction is not measured by physical distance. It is measured by the fractures in your attention, the quiet erosion of presence through a thousand minor departures that do not look like leaving. You believe you are balancing responsibility, ambition, and love with admirable effort. What you are actually doing is scattering your attention so thinly that nothing receives the fullness of you, not even the moments you insist matter most. Distraction convinces you that half presence is still presence, that sitting in the chair counts as being part of what is happening right in front of you.

Gloria Mark, a psychologist and informatics researcher whose work focuses on human attention, exposes the cost hidden inside every glance at your phone.[37] Each shift in focus leaves cognitive residue, a drag on your ability to reenter the moment. Her studies show that after a single digital interruption, it can take several minutes for your mind to settle fully again. When these micro disruptions pile up dozens or hundreds of times a day, your attention never fully returns. You live in a state of partial departure, always slightly removed from your own life. The cost remains invisible until you realize you cannot remember the last time you were fully present anywhere.

Distraction rarely feels like a choice. It feels like a current you cannot resist, a tide that pulls you out of the moment before you realize you have drifted. But underneath the pull is a point of decision you keep missing. The moment where presence is still available and distraction is still optional, even when it does not feel optional at all. The moment is small and easy to overlook, which is why most people do not recognize they had a choice until the consequences appear on the faces of the people who stopped expecting their full attention.

Attention is experienced as care. Inattention is experienced as distance. This is how distraction rewrites your relationships without your awareness. Children learn not to expect your eyes. Partners shorten their stories because they can feel you slipping. Friends keep conversations shallow because depth requires attention you cannot sustain. You are not withdrawing on purpose. You are surviving in a world that trains you to live everywhere except here. But intention does not change impact. The space between you and the people you love widens quietly until they adapt to your unavailability while you continue believing you are showing up. Presence is not about where your body sits. Presence is about where your attention lives, and when your mind is elsewhere, your life begins to live elsewhere too.

Why We Can't Stay Present

Most people assume distraction happens because they are failing at focus. They treat presence as a discipline problem, a matter of willpower or better habits or a less demanding life. But presence feels difficult for a different reason. Your nervous system has adapted to a rhythm of constant stimulation. When your attention shifts hundreds of times a day, your body learns to perceive motion as safety and stillness as threat. Quiet moments feel foreign, sometimes even unsafe, so your mind reaches for escape. The pull toward distraction isn't weakness, it's conditioning. Your brain has been trained to treat rapid input as normal, which makes the slower pace of presence feel uncomfortable even when you long for it.

Research by Adam Gazzaley, a neurologist and cognitive neuroscientist, shows that our ancient brains have strict limits on attention and were never built to juggle multiple information streams at modern speed without consequence.[38] Each time you shift tasks, you create interference that lingers and makes it harder to return fully to what you were doing before. What feels like multitasking is actually rapid task switching, and each switch degrades the fidelity of what you're doing. The more often you bounce between messages, tabs, and thoughts, the more your brain begins to prefer novelty over depth, as frequent switching provides a constant hit of new stimulation that the reward system learns to seek out. Presence asks you to stay with one experience long enough for your mind to settle. Distraction offers a steady drip of stimulation that feels easier in the moment even as it hollows out your capacity for connection. Over time, your attention becomes optimized for movement rather than meaning.

This is why presence feels heavier than it really is. Staying where you are means noticing what you usually miss. The boredom. The ambiguity. The emotional shifts in someone's voice. The way a child looks at you before deciding whether to speak. Presence requires contact with reality in its unedited form. Distraction protects you from that contact by letting you drift before anything becomes too real. It is easier to check a message than to register disappointment on someone's face. Easier to scroll than to sit with the discomfort of being needed. Distraction doesn't lighten what's happening. It only hides it long enough to create distance that feels unintentional but slowly becomes familiar.

The longer this pattern continues, the more it reshapes your identity. You start believing you are someone who cannot focus or someone incapable of being fully present. But this isn't who you are. It's who you became while adapting to a world that rewards responsiveness over depth, speed over engagement, presence in fragments instead of presence in full. Your scattered attention is not evidence of personal failure. It's the imprint of a nervous system trained to divide itself. Distraction is not your nature, it's your conditioning. And presence becomes possible the moment you recognize that what was learned can be unlearned.

Reclaiming Your Attention

When Eli finally looked up from his phone and felt the distance in his daughter's eyes, something inside him shifted. He realized he could not repair what he kept missing by promising himself he would try harder. Presence would not appear through intention alone. It required a different way of showing up. The next week at practice, he did something he had not done in years. He turned his phone off completely and left it in the glove compartment of his car. The silence felt unnatural at first, like stepping into a room with nothing in it. He felt restless. His mind reached for familiar stimulation and found nothing to grab. In that empty space, something unexpected began to happen. His attention started to settle.

Presence is not a feeling, it's a skill. It begins with a single choice to remain with what is in front of you even when your mind wants to run. Eli sat on the sideline and let the discomfort rise and fall without responding to it. He watched the way Ivy scanned the field. He heard the sound of the ball against cleats. He felt a small tug in his chest when she looked toward him and clearly did not expect him to be paying attention. He stayed anyway. He did not analyze the moment or try to make it meaningful. He simply remained long enough for the noise inside him to quiet on its own.

As the minutes passed, something softened. Nothing dramatic happened. The moment did not swell with emotion or reveal something profound. It simply became real. Eli saw his daughter more clearly than he had in months, not because she had changed but because he had stopped leaving before the moment reached him. He noticed how she celebrated a teammate's save. The way she adjusted her ponytail between plays. Small details he would have missed if his attention had been elsewhere. Presence began as a choice he made for her. It quickly became a choice he realized he needed for himself.

When Both Options Serve the Moment

There are moments when full presence is not possible or even wise. Moments when your nervous system is overwhelmed, when a situation demands rapid response, or when temporary distraction protects you from becoming emotionally flooded. Stepping away so your system can settle is not avoidance. It's care. The key is whether distraction is a conscious pause or an unconscious escape. Neuroscientist Mary Helen Immordino-Yang, whose research explores how emotions, learning, and the brain's default mode interact, has shown that the mind needs alternating periods of focus and inward drift in order to process experience, regulate emotion, and form meaning.[39] The brain requires time to turn inward through mind wandering, reflection, and story making to integrate what you've lived and support healthy regulation. Presence is strengthened by intentional rest. Allowing the mind to wander in a chosen way restores your ability to return with clarity rather than depletion.

The boundary is intention. Healthy distraction carries a planned return. It creates space for your system to regulate so you can reenter the moment with your full attention. Unconscious distraction has no return built into it. It pulls you away before you even register what you need. When Eli began practicing presence, he learned to notice which moments called for his full awareness and which required stepping back first so he could come back more fully. He discovered that presence is not rigid immersion. It grows through rhythm. Attention followed by rest. Engagement followed by recovery. This pattern allowed him to meet his life with steadiness rather than scattering himself across every demand.

Presence becomes most powerful when you stop treating it as an all-or-nothing state and begin treating it as a relationship with your own attention. Some situations need your full awareness. Others need a breath before that awareness becomes available. Discernment is the quiet skill that tells the difference. The meta-skill is not simply focus or productivity. It is the choice to inhabit the life unfolding in front of you rather than the endless elsewhere your distractions keep offering. Your attention is finite. Where it lives is where your life lives.

Where This Choice Shows Up Every Day

Work. A colleague asks for your input during a meeting and your eyes drift to your email. Distraction makes multitasking feel efficient while leaving you absent from the room. Presence closes the screen and returns your attention to the person speaking. The conversation becomes clearer because you are actually there for it.

Romantic Relationships. Your partner begins sharing something vulnerable and your phone lights up with a message that feels urgent. Distraction tells you to check it quickly, creating a small fracture in connection. Presence places the phone aside and stays with their tone, their expression, the meaning beneath their words. Closeness replaces another moment of feeling unseen.

Parenting. Your child tells you about their day while you scroll without noticing. Distraction looks like listening, but it isn't. Presence sets the phone down and meets their eyes long enough to hear the story they are offering. The shift is subtle but profound. Their voice steadies because they feel seen and heard.

Friendship. A friend shares something important during lunch and your mind slips to the list of things you need to finish later. Distraction rehearses tasks while their words drift past. Presence returns to the conversation and listens for what they are actually trying to say. Depth replaces surface because you are responding to a real person rather than to your own internal noise.

Everyday Tasks. You stand in line at the grocery store and instinctively reach for your phone to fill the quiet. Distraction turns every small pause into something to escape. Presence allows the stillness, notices your breath, the people around you, the simplicity of where you are. The task does not change. The texture of your day does. Life begins to meet you instead of rushing past you.

Practice Exercises: The FENCE Method

Presence doesn't require perfect focus or eliminating all distraction. These practices help you build a boundary around the moment, notice when your attention has slipped through, and find your way back before absence becomes distance.

F – Follow One Thread. Every moment contains many threads and your mind wants to chase all of them. Choose one. A voice. A gesture. A sentence beginning. A feeling rising in your chest. Let that single thread guide your attention. When your mind wanders, return to it. Presence begins with choosing one thing worth staying for.

E – Establish a Touchpoint. Presence needs somewhere to land. Pick a physical or relational anchor that keeps you from drifting. The warmth of your hand resting on your leg. The steadiness of someone's eyes. The sensation of a breath deep in your body. A touchpoint is not a grounding trick. It is a point of contact that holds you inside the moment.

N – Name What Is Happening. Quietly describe what is happening right now in simple language. *I am listening. I am watching. I am here with my child.* Naming brings your awareness out of the imagined future or the recycled past and into the exact place your life is unfolding. Words turn the abstract present into a lived experience.

C – Close the Loop. When distraction pulls you away, acknowledge your return. Reenter the moment with a sentence that reconnects you. *Tell me the part I missed. Keep going. I am with you now.* These small repairs prevent micro absences from becoming emotional distance and remind your mind that presence is always recoverable.

E – Experience the Shift. Stay long enough for something to register. A change in someone's voice. A softening in your own breath. A brief moment of understanding. Presence is not about intensity. It is about allowing what is happening to leave an imprint on you. That shift is your quiet proof that you were truly here.

When You Stop Missing It

Three months after the morning he missed Ivy's goal, Eli stood on the sidelines of another game, but everything about him felt different. He arrived early as he always did, yet the familiar restlessness that once sent him searching for distraction never appeared. His phone stayed in the glove compartment of his car, not because he forced himself to leave it there, but because he no longer wanted it near what he had learned was too easy to lose. When Ivy ran onto the field, he watched her with a steadiness he had never allowed himself before. He noticed the way she tied her cleats twice when she felt nervous. The way she scanned the sideline to find him. The small smile she gave when she realized he was fully there and not somewhere else inside his mind.

The change was not dramatic. There was no grand apology or sudden reinvention. Instead, it arrived through dozens of small adjustments that quietly reshaped how he lived. He stopped answering messages during dinner. He closed his laptop when Ivy walked into the room instead of promising himself he would finish one more thing. He listened more than he spoke, not to perform better parenting, but because he realized he had missed the sound of her thoughts. Presence softened something in him that distraction had held tight. It slowed him down enough to feel his own life instead of rushing past it.

The most surprising change appeared in the quietest moments. Standing in the kitchen making breakfast. Sitting beside Ivy while she finished homework. Walking the dog at night. He began to feel something he did not recognize at first. It was ease. The weight he had carried from living in a constant state of partial awareness began to lift. He could feel the difference between being alive and being present, and it startled him how long he had confused the two. There comes a point when you recognize the cost of drifting through the days you meant to live. When you understand that attention is not just a habit. It's the way you love people. It's the way you build meaning. It's the way your life becomes yours again. Presence does not demand perfection. It simply asks you to return before the moments meant to hold you move on without you.

13

Reaction or Response

the split second that changes everything

Maya had rehearsed this presentation thirty-three times. She practiced in front of her bathroom mirror, during morning runs, while waiting for her coffee to brew. This was her moment. Five years rebuilding her career after a divorce that nearly broke her. Five years proving she could excel at work even while her personal life fell apart. The VP of Strategy decision would follow this presentation, and Maya had earned the chance through sheer endurance and countless nights when sleep felt optional. Her phone was on Do Not Disturb. Her slides were flawless. Her navy suit made her feel steady and sharp. At exactly 10:00 a.m., the leadership team filed in. Maya smiled, made eye contact, and felt confidence rising as she opened with the market analysis she had perfected over three weeks. Her voice was steady. Her hands weren't shaking. She was hitting every mark.

Then the buzz. The distinct vibration that meant someone had overridden her Do Not Disturb settings. Only two people could do that. Her 12-year-old daughter Emma and her ex-husband. Maya glanced at the screen mid-sentence. The message glowed like a warning flare. "Emergency with Emma. Call me NOW." From David. The man who had turned their three-year divorce into psychological warfare. The man who called everything an emergency. A ten-minute delay at pickup.

A permission slip he hadn't seen. Anything less than an A on a test. He had used their daughter as leverage so often that Maya had learned to expect manipulation disguised as crisis. But what if this time was real?

Her mouth went dry. Her heart pounded so loudly she could hear it in her ears. Her breath turned shallow, her chest tightening as if something heavy had pressed down on it. The metallic taste of fear filled her tongue. Her thoughts spun into catastrophic images before she could stop them. Car accident. Hospital. School lockdown. The phrase "emergency with Emma" looped through her mind, each repetition pulling her further from the room. Her vision narrowed. The faces in front of her blurred as tunnel vision took over. Her body issued its command with brutal certainty. *Drop everything. Go now.* She knew this surge. It was the same one that once pulled her out of meetings when David said Emma had a fever of ninety-nine degrees. The same one that made her abandon a client dinner because he claimed Emma was crying over math homework. The same one that cost her the Johnson account when she fled a pitch meeting after he texted that Emma had scraped her cheek at the playground. Each time, her reaction felt justified. Each time, she learned later that the crisis had been exaggerated or invented.

Now, standing in front of the leadership team, Maya felt herself on the edge of shattering. One more second and she would stop mid-sentence, abandon the room, sabotage the opportunity she had spent five years rebuilding her life for. She stood at a choice point that exists in every triggering moment, though most people never see it. In the next breath, she would either let panic make the decision for her or she would find a way to stay in the room long enough to choose her response instead of being carried by her reaction. She had no idea that what happened in this half-second would shape far more than a single presentation. It would determine whether she spent the rest of her life whipped around by every crisis, every trigger, every signal that felt urgent but might not be. The difference between those two paths had nothing to do with willpower. It had everything to do with something she had never been taught to notice. There is always a space between what happens to you and what you do next.

Why Your Choice Matters

Here is the truth that will change how you handle every difficult moment. You are not your first reaction. Even when it feels like you are. Especially when it feels like you are. Most people believe their emotional explosions are automatic, inevitable, part of their nature. Someone criticizes you and you defend instantly. Your teenager gives you attitude and you snap back before thinking. Your boss sends a passive-aggressive email and your blood pressure spikes as if on cue. It feels unavoidable. What else could happen? But between what happens and how you respond, there is always space. Always. Even when you cannot see it. Even when it feels like there is no choice. Even when you are convinced your reaction is simply who you are.

Viktor Frankl, an Austrian psychiatrist and Holocaust survivor, described discovering this inner space under conditions most of us cannot imagine.[40] In the concentration camps, he lost his family, his home, and every freedom except one. The freedom to choose how he responded inside his own mind. His insight was not abstract philosophy. It was lived reality. If that space existed for him amid brutality, it certainly exists in your Monday meeting, during the argument in your kitchen, or in the e-mails in your inbox. Each time you react without choosing, you reinforce the belief that you cannot choose. Each unconscious explosion becomes evidence that you are wired this way: too emotional, too reactive, unable to handle pressure. You are not discovering your limitations. You are rehearsing them until they feel like truth.

The difficulty is that this space is easy to miss. When your alarm system activates, whether through criticism, conflict, bad news, or sudden change, your innate wiring takes over faster than thought. You know this moment. You feel yourself reacting and cannot stop it. Your heart races. Your thinking fogs. You say things you do not mean. Make decisions you regret. Act in ways that do not match who you want to be. Psychologist Daniel Goleman, who helped popularize the concept of emotional intelligence, calls this an amygdala hijack, the moment when the brain's threat system overrides rational thought and triggers an outsized emotional reaction.[41] You experience it as being yanked around by your emotions. That is reaction. Automatic, unconscious, designed for survival in a world where threats were physical and immediate. Response is something else entirely. Response happens when you enter the space between trigger and action and intentionally use it. When you catch yourself before you explode. When you breathe before you speak. When you choose your next move instead of being carried by fear or anger.

Maya found this space that morning. Instead of bolting from the room, she took one conscious breath and made a choice. She told herself she would finish the presentation with excellence and then address whatever was happening with steadiness rather than panic. Twenty minutes later she called her ex back and learned that the emergency was Emma falling off her bike and scraping her knee. His definition of crisis was her daughter needing a bandage. If Maya had reacted instead of responding, she would have sabotaged her biggest career moment over a minor injury.

Why We Mistake Speedy Reactions for Safety

When something triggers strong emotion, your brain's attention system makes an immediate decision about where to direct your resources. This system evolved to prioritize urgent threats over thoughtful analysis because survival once depended on reacting first and understanding later. If the shadow in your peripheral vision was a predator, the person who paused to evaluate the situation often did not survive. Speed became safety. Your brain detects potential danger and floods your body with stress chemicals in milliseconds, long before your rational mind catches up. Your heart pounds as blood rushes to your muscles. Your breathing turns rapid and shallow. Your thinking becomes cloudy as oxygen shifts from your prefrontal cortex to your limbs, preparing you to act. The system that kept your ancestors alive now undermines your modern life.

Your brain cannot distinguish between a charging lion and a challenging email from your mother-in-law. It treats psychological threats like criticism, rejection, conflict, and embarrassment with the same alarm it would use for physical attack.[42] When this alarm system takes over, you lose access to your best thinking. Blood flow decreases to the regions responsible for reasoning, creativity, and emotional regulation. You become temporarily less capable, which is why you say and do things during conflict that make no sense to you later. Modern culture amplifies this malfunction. Constant notifications fragment your attention and train your brain to expect interruption. Work environments reward speed over depth. Fast replies signal commitment. Quick decisions look like leadership. Immediate reactions are praised as engagement.

In these environments, slowing down feels like failure even when that is exactly what the moment requires.

You know the alarm system has taken over the instant you feel heat move through your body. When your voice changes pitch and pace. When your focus narrows to the problem in front of you and everything else fades. It is the sickening sensation of watching yourself escalate something you do not want to escalate, feeling unable to stop. Sometimes this wiring serves you perfectly. You pull your child back from traffic without hesitation. You rush toward someone who is hurt. You duck before you consciously register what is flying toward you. These are moments when ancient instincts protect you. But the same system becomes a trap when it treats everyday stress as emergency. You snap at your family because work was overwhelming. You send reactive messages that create new problems. You make major decisions while flooded with chemicals that distort your perception. The wiring designed to save your life now quietly sabotages it.

Claiming the Pause

Response lives in the space between trigger and action. It's the pause before you speak when you are angry. The breath you take when someone pushes your buttons. The moment you catch yourself about to explode and instead ask, "What does this situation actually need from me?" This feels impossible when your alarm system takes over because your body reacts as though immediate action is the only safe choice. Your entire system argues for moving fast, for following the familiar pathway of attack, defend, or escape. But response offers something reaction cannot. The power to act from your values instead of your fears. Your fear is not wrong. Your obedience to it is. The alarm system telling you there is danger is doing exactly what it was designed to do. The problem is letting that alarm make every decision for you.

When you respond instead of react, your behavior emerges from who you want to be rather than what your panicked mind believes will protect you. You speak from love instead of hurt. You make decisions based on what actually matters instead of what feels urgent in the moment. You do not need months of training to access this space. You only need to learn to recognize the moment of choice. Response looks like Maya staying present with her presentation while acknowledging her trigger, then addressing the situation with calm competence rather than frantic assumption. It appears when your teenager gives you attitude, and instead of immediately snapping back, you pause long enough to remember they are struggling with their own stress and what they need is connection, not correction. It happens when your partner says something that stings and instead of attacking or withdrawing, you take a breath and say, "That hit me hard. Can we talk about what is really happening here?" It emerges when someone cuts you off in traffic and instead of exploding into rage, you notice your anger, take a breath, and remember their driving has nothing to do with your worth as a human being.

The invitation is not to eliminate emotional activation. Your emotions provide essential information about what matters to you, what boundaries need attention, and what values are being threatened. The invitation is to use that emotional information as data for wise action rather than fuel for automatic reaction.

When Both Options Serve the Moment

Not every moment requires you to slow down. Some require the precision of instinct. Others need the steadiness of deliberate choice. Genuine emergencies demand immediate reaction. When your child bolts toward traffic, when someone collapses, when danger is unmistakably physical and immediate, your nervous system's speed becomes the right tool. Do not pause to reflect in those moments. But these situations are far rarer than your daily sense of urgency suggests. Most of what feels critical in ordinary life is not. The argument with your partner, the sharp email from your boss, the unexpected text, the family tension, the social media comment. These moments feel like they demand speed, but they actually need space.

The key distinction is time. Real emergencies unfold in seconds and require immediate action. Everything else gives you the gift of a pause, even three breaths, in which a different choice becomes possible. The text Maya received felt like a crisis, but it wasn't. Most "urgent moments" aren't. The hard conversation with your spouse can wait long enough for you to get centered. The criticism from your boss can be met with clarity instead of defense. The family conflict can sit still long enough for understanding to surface. What matters is what you do with the time you actually have. The meta-skill is learning to notice the space between impact and action, and choosing the version of you that should step into the moment. Response emerges when your emotional signals and your thinking mind work together, emotion showing you what matters, and perspective showing you what to do with it. That collaboration is what allows you to act from intention rather than impulse.

Where This Choice Shows Up Every Day

Heated Conversations. Someone says something that lands harder than it should and touches an old bruise you thought had healed. Reaction fires back with sarcasm, hurt, or silence because it feels safer to protect yourself than to stay open. Response pauses long enough to notice the wound beneath the moment, to understand both their meaning and your own pain, and chooses engagement that strengthens the relationship instead of feeding the ego.

Parenting Moments. Your child melts down, defies a rule, or tests every limit at the worst possible time. Reaction meets their chaos with yelling, threats, or withdrawal because your nervous system mirrors theirs. Response slows the exchange just enough to see what they actually need, whether connection, containment, or guidance, and acts from steadiness rather than exhaustion.

Professional Pressure. A deadline collapses, criticism blindsides you, or someone challenges you in front of others. Reaction defends, deflects, or spirals into catastrophic thinking. Response takes a breath, separates what is true from what only feels personal, and chooses action that supports the career you are building rather than the comfort you crave. The moment shifts from threat to information, and from panic to possibility.

Technology and Traffic. The screen freezes, a driver swerves into your lane, or the phone dies at the worst time. Reaction erupts in frustration and lets irritation dictate the rest of your day. Response acknowledges the annoyance without surrendering the emotional landscape to it, remembering that one inconvenience does not decide the quality of the day ahead.

Family Dynamics. Your mother repeats the same comment she has made for thirty years. A sibling revives an old rivalry. A holiday gathering awakens patterns you thought you had outgrown. Reaction collapses into the familiar through defensiveness, withdrawal, or attack. Response recognizes the trigger as something from the past and chooses behavior aligned with who you are now rather than who you were then. This is how generational cycles quietly end.

Practice Exercises: The SPACE Protocol

Reaction feels instant because it is. These practices help you catch the surge before it takes over, create room between what triggered you and what you do next, and choose a response that aligns with who you want to be instead of who the moment is trying to make you become.

S – Stop. The moment you notice emotional activation, whether tension in your body or urgency in your mind, stop for one conscious breath. Not a long pause, just a single intentional inhale that interrupts the automatic spiral and creates the first inch of room for choice. That inch is where clarity begins.

P – Physical Check. Scan your body for alarm signals. Tight jaw. Clenched fists. Shallow breathing. Racing heart. These cues tell you exactly when your ancient protective system has taken over, giving you information about your emotional state before you speak or act. Your body often recognizes activation long before your mind does.

A – Ask the Question. Ask quietly "What does this situation actually need from me?" This question interrupts the pull of reactivity and reconnects you to context. It shifts your focus from the emotional charge to the larger truth of the moment, which often reveals that urgency is not the same as importance.

C – Choose Your Values. Identify how you want to show up. What would integrity look like here? What would courage say? What response would allow you to feel proud of yourself an hour from now? Values create direction when emotions try to dictate speed.

E – Execute Consciously. Take action from this grounded state rather than from your initial emotional surge. The response might be setting a boundary, asking for clarification, taking a break, or choosing silence, but it emerges from intention rather than instinct. Conscious action is how you reclaim the moment and yourself within it.

Mastering the Split Second

Maya got the VP position. Not because she stopped feeling fear when David texted her, but because she showed she could stay present when every part of her wanted to flee. She learned that her ex-husband's panic no longer dictated her behavior. More importantly, she discovered that the same space that saved her presentation was available in every difficult moment, in every conversation, in every decision.

You discover the same truth as this practice becomes yours. Dialogues that once dissolved into defensiveness become opportunities for clarity. Conflicts that once spiraled become moments of repair. Relationships grow because people feel safe with your steadiness. Opportunities expand because you are no longer driven by urgency. Children learn emotional regulation by watching you model it. Your life begins to align with what matters because your choices emerge from a sense of presence rather than impulse. Every time you find the space between trigger and action, you reclaim one of the most profound human capacities: the ability to choose your response rather than letting old patterns choose for you. This choice determines whether conflict escalates or resolves, whether relationships deepen or erode, whether challenges become growth or evidence that you are overwhelmed, and whether you act from your highest values or your oldest wounds.

Most importantly, you stop being pulled into other people's chaos. The button someone used to press no longer guarantees a predictable reaction. The person who once controlled your emotions no longer gets automatic access to them. You become a source of calm not because nothing affects you, but because you have learned how to stay with yourself when something does. Your willingness to use this space becomes the foundation for authentic connection, meaningful work, genuine confidence, and a steadiness that does not disappear in difficulty. The person who learns to pause becomes the person who leads their life instead of being dragged through it by reflex. You can keep surrendering to every trigger, living at the mercy of your history, or you can reclaim the space between what happens and what you choose next. That space is smaller than a heartbeat, yet powerful enough to change the course of your life.

14

Resentment or Release

the story that won't let go

Marcus's hands were already shaking before he lifted the envelope, and he hated himself for it. The cream-colored cardstock with the embossed lettering sat on his desk like something he had been bracing for months. "Jasmine & Tucker's Bundle of Joy!" Tiny footprints. A photo of his younger sister standing in a field of wildflowers, belly rounding under her dress. Marcus had spent weeks hoping she might keep the shower small and spare him this particular hit. His chest tightened as he read the date. Two months away. Saturday afternoon. No excuse believable enough, no way to decline without exposing the rawness he had spent three years trying to hide.

Three years ago, Marcus and his husband Daniel had started trying to build their family. Three years later, they were still suspended in the same cycle of hope, paperwork, and disappointment. Intake meetings where agencies delivered polite versions of "not a fit." Consultations explaining why certain paths were possible in theory but nearly unworkable in practice. Conversations about timelines that stretched into years. Nights when the grief hit without warning, grief that had no clear shape, no medical category, no moment when anyone said it was reasonable to stop hoping. They had painted a nursery early on when optimism still felt safe. Now the room sat empty, a quiet reminder of everything they could not bring home.

Meanwhile, Jasmine had gotten pregnant without trying. Eighteen months married. One casual "We weren't really trying." And it happened. No stalled processes. No closed doors. No savings drained by consultations that led nowhere. Just morning sickness posts on Instagram with soft filters and hashtags about being blessed. Marcus had watched every update. The ultrasound showing tiny developing fingers. The gender reveal with pink smoke drifting across their backyard. The nursery progress featuring a crib he could not afford because his own savings had been redirected into paths that kept collapsing. Each notification felt like another twist in a wound he still checked compulsively, the same way someone watches a tanking market even when looking does nothing to change the outcome.

The hardest moments were the ones that revealed something darker inside him. When Jasmine wrote about being overwhelmed or afraid, Marcus felt a brief, shameful flicker of satisfaction. *See? It is not all perfect.* That thought humiliated him, and the humiliation made the resentment worse. He loved his sister. He had defended her from middle school bullies. He had walked her down the aisle when their father could not. Now he couldn't look at a photo of her without his jaw tightening and his stomach twisting with something uncomfortably close to rage. The embossed lettering on the invitation blurred as tears returned. His client's deposition started in twenty minutes, and he was crying again at his desk over a baby shower.

He set the invitation down gently, as if roughness might expose something he was not ready to face. He could already imagine himself at the shower, smiling so hard his jaw ached, buying a gift that cost more than it should so he could signal grace he did not feel, listening to nursery themes and birth plans while his own dream stayed stalled in a process that felt endless. Every part of him wanted to text Jasmine a polite excuse. But

Daniel's words from therapy still echoed in his mind. "What if this is not really about Jasmine having something you want? What if it is grief you have not let yourself feel?" The real decision was not about the RSVP. It was about whether he would keep letting resentment corrode the relationship he loved, or allow himself to feel the grief without turning it into a moral indictment against his sister. Whether he could walk into that shower and let all of it be true at the same time, the love, the sorrow, the unfairness, without needing any of it to cancel the rest.

Why Your Choice Matters

The story plays on repeat in your mind like a song you cannot turn off. What they said at Thanksgiving three years ago. How they dismissed your pain. The way they got the promotion you believed should have been yours. You have replayed it so many times you could recite it backward, every detail vivid while other memories fade. This is no longer remembering what happened. This is tending a wound you refuse to let heal, rehearsing a script about being wronged until it becomes the lens through which you see everything. The resentment feels righteous, almost like evidence you are gathering for a judgment that never arrives. But what you are calling justice is really a way of keeping yourself stuck, and you are the one who pays the cost.

Frederic Luskin, a clinical psychologist and director of the Stanford Forgiveness Projects, spent decades studying forgiveness, and his findings challenge most assumptions about letting go.[43] Forgiveness does not mean excusing the harm or pretending the pain was small. It does not require reconciliation or renewed closeness with someone who has shown they cannot be trusted. Forgiveness is the act of releasing the story's hold on you so your energy can return to the parts of your life that are still unfolding. Luskin's research shows that people who grip resentment experience higher levels of anxiety, depression, and stress-related illness. The damage does not come from the original event, which ended long ago. It comes from the ongoing rehearsal, a quiet self-punishment the person who hurt you will never feel. They may have moved on without a second thought. You are the one paying the cost.

Resentment survives on a simple illusion. You believe your continued suffering balances the scales. You believe replaying the injury proves something about their guilt. You believe releasing your anger would mean they win and you lose. But resentment does not hurt them. It does not teach them anything, change anything, or make anything right. It only transforms a finite injury into an injury with no endpoint. Choosing release does not erase what happened. It simply declares that the past will not be allowed to dictate the entire arc of your future. It recognizes that this story, however justified, no longer protects you. It confines you. And the cost of continuing to carry it has grown larger than the original wound ever was.

Why We Refuse to Let Go

When someone hurts you deeply, whether intentionally or through thoughtless action, holding onto that hurt can feel like the only power you have left. You could not control what they did, but you can control how long you remember it, how carefully you catalogue it, and how fully you let it shape the story of what happened. Resentment becomes a form of agency in a moment that made you feel powerless. It insists that they do not get to hurt you and walk away unchanged. Your continued anger feels like proof that the wound matters, that you matter, that this wrong cannot simply fade into the background. Resentment gives your pain a place to live when you do not know where else to put it. It turns helplessness into conviction, and conviction often feels easier to hold than vulnerability.

This habit formed when you truly had no other tools. As a child navigating unfairness or cruelty, you could not change the circumstances or protect yourself the way an adult can. Holding onto the belief that they were wrong and you were right became a lifeline. Resentment protected your sense of worth when the world around you did not. It allowed you to survive what you could not escape. But what protected you then now limits you. You are no longer powerless. You have the ability to choose how you interpret experiences and how you respond to the people who hurt you. Yet your mind still runs the old script: hold the evidence, rehearse the injury, make sure the story stays sharp. The strategy that once kept you intact now keeps you stuck.

Charlotte vanOyen Witvliet, a psychologist who has run a series of psychophysiology studies on unforgiveness and forgiving responses, studied what happens inside the body when people revisit grudges compared to when they practice forgiveness.[44] When participants imagined the person who hurt them, their bodies reacted as if facing an immediate threat. Blood pressure rose. Heart rate accelerated. Muscles tensed. Stress hormones flooded their systems and stayed elevated long after the imagining ended. The body cannot distinguish between remembering past harm and encountering present danger. Each time you replay the memory, your nervous system behaves as though the event is happening again. The resentment does not live only in your thoughts. It shows up in chronic tension, elevated cortisol, reduced immunity, and increased cardiovascular strain. You are not simply recalling what hurt you. You are reliving it inside a body that pays the full cost, while the person who caused the original pain remains unaffected.

Choosing Peace Over Proof

Release does not come from suppressing your feelings or pretending the story should feel better than it does. It begins when you stop needing the past to be different. Three weeks after Marcus received the baby shower invitation, he finally called Jasmine. Not to RSVP, but to tell her the truth he had been carrying in silence. "I need to be honest about something," he said. "I have been a terrible brother. Not because of what I have done, but because of what I have been feeling." He told her everything. The resentment. The obsessive monitoring of her posts. The shameful flicker of satisfaction when she admitted feeling scared. The way her joy had started to feel like confirmation of his own failure. When he finished, Jasmine was quiet. Then she said something that cracked him open. "I knew. I could feel the distance. It made me stop wanting to share things with you, which hurt because you are my brother."

Steven Hayes, a clinical psychologist and co-founder of Acceptance and Commitment Therapy (ACT), explains through his research on psychological flexibility exactly what Marcus discovered in that moment.[45] Psychological flexibility is the capacity to feel difficult emotions without letting them dictate your behavior, to hold your story gently enough that you remember it is a story and not the whole truth of your life. Hayes found that rigidity keeps people locked inside suffering. The more you insist that reality should unfold differently, the more tightly the pain wraps around you. Flexibility creates the space where healing can begin. Marcus could not change the fact that Jasmine conceived easily while he and Daniel faced barriers that had nothing to do with desire or readiness. That truth would remain. What could change was his relationship to the truth. He could acknowledge his grief without placing it on her shoulders. He could feel the unfairness without needing her joy to shrink in order for his pain to feel legitimate.

By the end of the call, Marcus had agreed to attend the shower. Not because his sadness had vanished, but because he no longer needed Jasmine's path to be difficult in order to survive his own. Release did not mean pretending everything was fine or ignoring the realities that shaped his struggle. It meant recognizing that resentment toward Jasmine changed nothing about the obstacles he faced and everything about the kind of brother he wanted to be. He discovered what everyone eventually learns when they choose release. You do not let go because someone deserves forgiveness. You let go because you deserve the peace that comes when the story stops running your life.

When Both Options Serve the Moment

Some boundaries may look like resentment from the outside but function as survival on the inside. When someone repeatedly violates your limits, when staying in the relationship requires tolerating ongoing harm, or when the pattern continues despite every attempt to address it, protecting yourself matters more than releasing your anger. Distance from people who hurt you is not punishment. It is protection. You can release the resentment while still holding firm boundaries. You can forgive someone and still decide they no longer have access to your life. Release does not require reconciliation or revisionist history. It simply means you refuse to let what they did take more from you than it already has.

Naming that something wrong happened, choosing not to trust someone who has shown they are untrustworthy, and creating boundaries rooted in reality all serve your well-being. Resentment becomes corrosive when the rehearsal of the wrong becomes your full-time occupation. When proving their flaws matters more than building the life you want. When the grievance evolves from something that happened to something you have become. If thinking about them occupies hours of your week, if you are still explaining their behavior years later, if your body tightens every time their name appears in conversation, the resentment has shifted from protection to poison.

Release begins to serve you when holding on costs more than letting go. It matters when the person who hurt you occupies space in your mind while having no awareness of your suffering. When your resentment spills into relationships that were never part of the original harm. When the past keeps stealing attention from the present. Most situations that feel like they demand resentment actually require clear boundaries and choices that reflect who you are now, not who you were when the injury occurred. You can remember what happened without replaying it. You can learn from the past without living inside it. You can acknowledge your pain without making it the center of your identity. The meta-skill is recognizing when a boundary protects you and when a resentment diminishes you, and understanding that peace is not weakness and letting go is not losing.

Where This Choice Shows Up Every Day

Family Wounds. Your father dismissed your pain years ago, and you have replayed that moment so often it feels present rather than past. Resentment keeps the injury alive, looping his words until they shape the entire relationship. Release allows you to name what happened without letting that moment define everything that came after. You stop waiting for him to become someone he has never been and begin choosing the relationship possible with who he is now.

Friendship Betrayals. A friend broke your trust in a way that shook you deeply, and every shared gathering still feels like a silent test of loyalty. Resentment turns the room into a place where you monitor every interaction, gathering proof that the hurt mattered. Release frees you from needing resolution. The friendship may not return, but your peace no longer relies on convincing anyone of what happened.

Professional Slights. A former boss took credit for your work, and you have carried that injustice like a weight you cannot put down. Resentment makes every workplace feel untrustworthy and every leader suspect. Release does not revise the history. It prevents the past from contaminating the future. You protect yourself through clarity and boundaries, not by tending a wound no one else remembers.

Romantic Endings. Someone you loved treated you carelessly, and part of you wants their life to mirror the pain they caused. Resentment keeps you checking for signs of struggle, tying your healing to their downfall. Release begins when you stop watching and stop comparing. You reclaim the energy invested in their consequences and direct it toward rebuilding your own life.

Daily Encounters. A driver cuts you off, a neighbor speaks thoughtlessly, a stranger snaps in passing. Resentment replays these small moments long after they end, collecting them as proof that the world is harsh. Release recognizes that most slights are thoughtless, not personal. You let them dissolve instead of letting them calcify into evidence.

Practice Exercises: Loosening the Grip

Resentment tightens gradually until you don't notice you're carrying it everywhere. These practices help you see what the grudge is costing you, interrupt the rehearsal before it becomes your default, and reclaim the energy you've been spending on a story that no longer serves you.

Resentment Inventory. Write down the specific grievance you find yourself returning to. Describe only what happened, when it happened, and what was said or done. Stay close to the facts of the moment rather than the story that formed afterward. Then note how many times the memory surfaced in the past week. When the number is high, the event itself is no longer what's being processed. The repetition is. This simple count is not about judgment or correctness. It clarifies whether something is still asking to be understood or whether it has shifted into rehearsal.

Cost Calculation. Divide a page into four sections: work, relationships, health, and personal growth. In each, name one way resentment has affected you. Avoid justification. Just name the impact. Missed conversations. Lost focus. Physical tension. Emotional withdrawal. Seeing the territory that resentment occupies changes the question you are asking. It is no longer who was right. It becomes whether holding this is worth what it is costing you.

Three Sentence Release. When you feel the familiar loop beginning, interrupt it with three sentences spoken aloud: *That happened. It hurt. I am choosing not to carry it today.* You are not denying the truth or minimizing the pain. You are reclaiming your attention. Tomorrow the same reminder may be needed again. That does not mean the practice failed. It simply means you are practicing.

Boundary Placement. Name one boundary that protects your steadiness going forward and put it in place without explanation or defense. You do not need agreement or understanding for a boundary to be valid. The boundary is not punishment. It is protection. Its purpose is to limit ongoing harm, not to prove a point or force acknowledgment.

Pattern Interrupt. Notice what reliably triggers the resentment spiral. When it appears, change your physical state. Stand up. Step outside. Shift rooms. Call someone grounding. The action itself matters less than breaking the automatic path back into rehearsal. Each interruption teaches your nervous system something new. This trigger no longer gets to decide what happens next.

The Weight That Lifts

Fourteen months after the shower, Marcus stood in Jasmine's backyard, watching his niece take unsteady steps across the grass. His chest tightened, but the feeling had shifted. It was no longer the dense pressure of resentment. It was a blend of grief for the story he longed to live and genuine happiness for the one Jasmine was living. The shower itself had been nearly unbearable. He bought a gift he could not afford, hid in the bathroom during waves of panic, and left with a headache that stayed for days. Yet when Jasmine later found him crying and simply sat beside him, something loosened. Therapy helped him turn inward rather than outward. He named grief about agencies that rejected them, anger at a system that favored one kind of family, fear that parenthood might never come. Naming those truths freed energy that resentment had trapped in place.

Six months later, a birth mother chose Marcus and Daniel. Their daughter was now three months old, and nothing about the journey had been simple. Still, Marcus learned something essential. Release did not erase grief. It meant his life was no longer defined by what he believed others had taken. When bitterness surfaced about the years spent waiting, he acknowledged it and then focused on the child in his arms. When pregnancy announcements appeared, he felt the familiar ache, allowed it to rise, and let it pass without turning it into a narrative. Release was not perfect or permanent. It was practiced one moment at a time, and over time the practice changed him.

Every time you choose release over resentment, you teach yourself that past wrongs no longer control present reality. This choice determines whether the next five years become a continuation of the grievance or the beginning of the life you want to build. Living in resentment means waking each morning with the same wound, watching others move forward while you remain anchored to what happened. Your relationships contract because everyone becomes potential evidence in a story that never ends. Your body carries the strain because resentment floods you with stress chemicals designed for brief emergencies rather than long-term residence. Your future narrows because the energy you could invest in creating something meaningful drains into maintaining a story that cannot change.

Living in release means accepting that the hurt was real while understanding that gripping it only restricts your capacity to be present for what is here now. Relationships deepen because people are no longer measured against past injuries. Opportunities widen because the weight of the old story no longer colors every exchange. Your body relaxes because your nervous system finally senses that the danger has passed. Release does not make you forgetful or naive. It makes you free. Free to set boundaries without bitterness. Free to remember without reliving. Free to build a life shaped by desire rather than grievance. The cost of holding on will always exceed whatever was taken from you. Release is not letting anyone win. It is choosing to stop losing yourself.

15

Someday or Today

the life that you keep postponing

Jamie had been driving past the brick art studio for almost a decade. Every morning she glanced toward its wide front windows where canvases leaned in casual stacks that looked like possibility disguised as clutter. She often pictured herself inside holding a brush or leaving with a painting still drying at the edges. The fantasy had grown familiar, even comforting, because imagining did not require courage. She always told herself that one day she would sign up for a class, but she had been saying one day for nine years without noticing how easily someday became a pattern. It felt responsible to wait until work slowed down or until she felt less embarrassed by wanting something without knowing if she had any talent. Beneath those reasonable explanations lived a quieter truth. Wanting deeply and acting on that desire were not the same thing, and she had learned how to want without ever letting it shape her life.

One Thursday evening she left the office long after the sun had set. Rain streaked across her windshield as she turned the familiar corner by the studio and noticed a sheet of paper taped to the inside of the front door. Through the blur of headlights and water she made out the words *Closing Next Month*. She pulled into the small parking lot before she fully understood what she was doing. Her hands trembled as she put the car in park. It surprised her how sharply the sight of that sign landed. She had imagined stepping into that studio for so long that the idea of it disappearing felt like losing a future she had been quietly relying on.

She turned off the engine and watched the rain soften against the glass. Inside, a woman moved through the space, stacking chairs and brushing flecks of dried paint into a neat pile. The scene was ordinary, but it struck Jamie with unexpected force. All her waiting rose at once. She thought about the years when she could barely afford rent, the stretch after her divorce when she felt hollowed out, the seasons when painting seemed like an indulgence she had not yet earned. She had told herself that timing mattered, that someday she would finally feel steady enough to begin. What she felt now was not fear. It was grief for the versions of herself she had postponed in the name of being practical.

The woman inside lifted a canvas from the wall and set it beside a stack of boxes. The simplicity of the gesture tightened Jamie's throat. She realized she had been living as though time were generous and guaranteed. She had treated someday like certainty instead of possibility. The sign in the window had not taken anything from her. It had revealed how fragile her assumptions had always been. The life she pictured living later required her presence now. Each year she had waited to feel ready had been a year she could have been learning, growing, becoming the person she imagined. The studio was closing, but what unsettled her most was the recognition that she had been closing the door on herself for years.

Jamie stepped out of the car without a plan, only a quiet refusal to keep trusting the version of herself who promised later. Cool air filled her lungs as she crossed the lot toward the door. She paused outside the studio, looking through the glass at the woman finishing her work for the night. The moment held the weight of two possible lives. One built on imagining. One built on beginning. She placed her hand on the handle and felt her heart answer before her thoughts could interfere.

Why Your Choice Matters

Most people believe they are delaying only an action, but what they are actually delaying is their life. Someday becomes an attractive refuge because it holds the promise of a future where you will feel more courageous or more deserving than you do right now. You picture a moment when things will be easier, when your schedule will open, when responsibilities will lighten. It feels mature to wait for that moment. It feels responsible to avoid disruption until you feel more stable. But beneath that quiet logic is an uncomfortable truth. Someday is rarely about timing, it's about safety. It protects you from the vulnerability of stepping into a life that will change you. You are not postponing an activity. You are postponing the part of yourself you hope will emerge once you feel ready to be seen.

Hal Hershfield, a psychologist who studies how people relate to their future selves, reveals through his research on future self-continuity why this pattern holds so much power.[46] He found that most people relate to their future selves the way they relate to strangers, familiar enough to recognize but distant enough to ignore. Many people's brains respond to their future self almost as if they were thinking about a different person, not the same individual extended through time. When you picture the future, you imagine a person who is calmer, braver, and more capable than you feel right now. The emotional distance between your present and future selves allows you to believe that the future you will do the things you are unwilling to do now. You assume they will have more time, more stability, and more clarity. But that future self never comes into existence unless you bring them into the present. They cannot act without you. They cannot become anything other than what your current choices train them to be. If you wait for courage now, they will wait too. If you postpone the life you want, they will inherit a life shaped entirely by postponement. The version of you who feels ready is a fantasy, not a reality.

The real choice is whether you will continue living inside the imagined safety of a future that never arrives or whether you will let your life begin in the imperfect conditions of today. Nothing dramatic announces the moment when someday becomes never. It happens quietly, in small rationalizations, in repeated promises that you will return later. You tell yourself you are not giving up on your dreams, you are simply waiting for the moment when everything will align. But alignment is not a moment. It is a decision. The question is not whether you are ready. It is whether you are willing to stop postponing the life that only exists when you choose to live it now.

Why We Postpone the Life We Want

Postponement is rarely about laziness or lack of discipline. It begins much earlier and much deeper than the explanations you give yourself. Most people were never taught how to live in real time. Instead, they learned instead how to manage expectations, stay within familiar routines, and avoid choices that might alter the shape of their lives too quickly. Someday becomes a psychologically comfortable place because it allows you to want something without having to risk anything. If you begin today, you might fail or succeed or be changed in ways you cannot predict. If you delay, you can keep the desire intact without confronting its consequences. The fear is not of taking a class or making a change. The fear is of stepping into a reality where imagination no longer protects you. Someday shields you from the emotional exposure of becoming someone new.

Irvin Yalom, an existential psychiatrist whose work explores how everyday life is quietly shaped by an underlying awareness of death and finitude, helps explain why this shield feels necessary.[47] He writes that beneath ordinary life runs a quiet awareness of time passing and an even quieter awareness that time is finite. When people brush against this truth, they do not always respond by seizing life. Often, they retreat. Choosing a path means accepting that other paths close. Committing to something meaningful introduces finality, and finality can feel threatening even when the choice is desired. The moment you choose today, you narrow the field of possibility that someday keeps wide open. Terror Management Theory shows that reminders of impermanence often push people toward routine, distraction, and delay rather than action.[48] Postponement becomes a buffer against the unsettling reality that every meaningful choice carries both opportunity and irreversibility.

This is why beginning in the present feels heavier than imagining the future. Today is concrete. Today has consequences. Today demands participation. Someday asks only for vision, and vision feels safer than embodiment. When you imagine a future where you finally feel brave or creative or free, you are not imagining a different world. You are imagining a different self, one untouched by hesitation or fear. That imagined version is easier to believe in than the real one standing here now. The moment you begin, that fantasy dissolves, and you are left with yourself in motion, imperfect and exposed. Postponement is not about time, it's about identity. You delay the life you want because stepping into it requires stepping out of the familiar self you have learned how to protect. It asks you to meet yourself not in theory, but in practice. And that encounter, more than any external obstacle, is what makes today feel so difficult to choose.

Choosing Today

Jamie did not walk into the studio because she felt brave. She walked in because she finally understood that waiting had not protected her. It had only kept her life suspended in possibility. Inside, the room smelled faintly of turpentine and clay. The woman stacking chairs looked up as Jamie asked about classes, her voice unsteady but sincere. There was no dramatic breakthrough, only a quiet willingness to let today matter. As the woman handed her a schedule, Jamie realized that the life she wanted had never required a wiser or more talented version of herself. It had required a present one, someone willing to be here rather than imagining a future where everything felt easier.

Developmental psychologist Robert Kegan's research on adult development reveals why this shift feels so profound.[49] He argues that real transformation happens when parts of your inner experience move from subject to object. Subject is what you're automatically "had by," the patterns so embedded in your thinking that you cannot see them as choices. Object is what you can see, reflect on, and choose about. What Jamie experienced was not just a behavioral choice, but what Kegan calls a transformation in her subject-object relationship. Someday had been subject for her, invisible and automatic. When she walked through that door, she moved someday from subject to object. She could finally see it for what it was, a protective story rather than an inevitable truth. Transformation is not about finding courage. It is about recognizing the stories you mistake for reality. This is why beginning feels so disorienting. You are not just changing what you do. You are changing the structure through which you understand who you are.

In the days after Jamie signed up, she noticed how often she used someday as a shield. She drove to her sister's house one evening with takeout instead of waiting for work to settle. She booked the weekend trip she had been mentally planning for years. She emailed a friend she kept meaning to reconnect with. None of these choices felt heroic, but each reminded her that the life she wanted would only form through participation, not imagination. Today is built through modest acts: the message you send while you still feel awkward, the class you attend though unsure of your place, the step you take without waiting for enthusiasm to arrive. Once Jamie stopped rehearsing who she hoped to become, she began living as someone who could grow.

When Both Options Serve the Moment

Not every dream belongs to today. Some pauses are acts of wisdom, giving your nervous system time to settle or your life time to stabilize before you can step forward. When you are grieving, when you are recovering from crisis, when your capacity is genuinely tender, delay can protect rather than avoid. The difference lives in what the pause creates. Wise delay has a name, a purpose, and a visible edge. It restores you so movement becomes possible again. Avoidance has none of these. It stretches without definition, quietly expanding until waiting becomes a way of being and someday turns into a place where nothing ever arrives.

Someday serves you when it honors real limitation and prepares the ground for future action. Today serves you when the life you want requires movement rather than more imagining, when delay no longer restores but slowly removes you from yourself. The work is learning to notice the shift. The moment waiting stops feeling spacious and starts feeling like distance from your own life. Your body registers this long before your mind is willing to admit it. The tightening in your chest when you hear yourself say *not yet* again. The dull heaviness that settles when another year passes and nothing has changed. These sensations are information. They are signals that postponement has crossed from care into quiet resignation.

Discernment is learning to tell the difference between waiting that honors your truth and waiting that hides your fear. It asks you to distinguish honest limitation from protective delay, and to recognize that the conditions you are waiting for may never fully arrive. The only time you ever actually get to inhabit your life is now. Presence is not about perfect timing or complete readiness. It is about engaging with what is here instead of negotiating endlessly with an imagined future. The meta-skill is not forcing yourself into action. It's recognizing when someday has become a story that keeps you suspended, and choosing to let today participate in shaping who you are becoming.

Where This Choice Shows Up Every Day

Work. You tell yourself you will apply for the new role once you finish one more training or feel more certain you are qualified. Someday softens the fear of being evaluated. Today submits the application even with uncertainty present. You discover that movement reveals possibilities preparation alone never uncovers.

Relationships. You delay reconnecting with someone you miss because you want the timing to feel right or the words to sound composed. Someday protects you from the vulnerability of being seen. Today sends the message or makes the call. You learn that closeness grows through presence, not through perfectly planned gestures.

Health. You imagine beginning a new habit when life slows down or motivation arrives. Someday disguises avoidance as discipline. Today takes a walk, cooks one nourishing meal, or stretches for five minutes. You realize your body responds to consistency, not imagined readiness.

Creativity. You picture starting a project once you have the ideal space, the perfect tools, or a clearer vision. Someday keeps desire intact but unreal. Today opens a notebook, mixes paint, or writes the first unpolished paragraph. You feel the grounding that comes from creating something that exists outside your mind.

Personal Growth. You wait to make changes until you feel more healed or more certain about the path ahead. Someday promises transformation without exposure. Today takes one small step toward the life you want while fear comes along for the ride. You experience the shift that only happens when you meet yourself in motion instead of imagination.

Practice Exercises: The Now Protocol

Someday feels safer than today because it never demands anything from you. These practices help you feel the true cost of deferral, recognize when delay has become a life strategy rather than a timeline, and take one action that proves today is the only moment you actually have.

The Mortality Minute. Set a timer for sixty seconds and imagine that everything in your life stays exactly as it is for the next ten years. No new experiences. No risks taken. Nothing claimed. Let yourself feel the emotional weight of that stillness without rushing to fix it. Most people discover that the fear of an unchanged life is heavier than the fear of beginning, and that this clarity arrives only when you stop numbing yourself with someday.

The Line of Two Lives. Draw two simple lines on a piece of paper. On the top line, write the life you are currently living through delay. On the bottom line, write the life that would begin to form if you stopped deferring one thing you want.

Do not list steps or goals. Describe the direction. Look at the divergence. Your life is already moving every day, with or without your consent. This exercise reveals that inaction is not neutral, it's a trajectory.

The Doorway Test. Whenever you catch yourself imagining a future moment where everything will feel easier, ask yourself what would change if today were the only chance you had. Not forever. Just today. If the answer is that you would act, then the obstacle has never been timing. It has been fear wearing the costume of patience. This question collapses fantasy and returns you to choice.

The Witnessing Walk. Take a ten-minute walk. Notice one thing you usually overlook: a sound, a color, a person's posture. Let your attention stay long enough for the moment to register. This practice is not about mindfulness for its own sake. It trains you to inhabit the day you are actually living instead of dissociating into imagined futures. You cannot choose today if you never feel yourself inside it.

The Small Declaration. Each morning, name one thing you will no longer defer, even if you only give it a moment of attention. Say it out loud. Declaring something anchors your intention in the present tense rather than the future. The action can be small. Five minutes. One message. One page. What matters is breaking the contract with later and reestablishing trust with now.

When Now Becomes Enough

Six months after Jamie stepped into the art studio, her life did not look dramatically different from the outside. She still worked long hours. She still paid bills on Thursdays. She still had evenings when she felt tired and unsure and tempted to fall back into old patterns. But something subtle and unmistakable had shifted. She no longer waited for life to feel easier before letting herself inhabit it. On Wednesday nights, she walked into a different studio across town because the first one had closed, and she painted beside people who did not care whether she was talented. She experienced the small, quiet joy of watching color move across a canvas without needing to prove anything. The change did not come from confidence. It came from choosing to be here instead of postponing herself until she felt worthy of participating.

Today began spreading in small, grounded ways. She visited her sister regularly without rehearsing the perfect moment. She took the weekend trip she had delayed for years and noticed how nourishing it felt to follow through on a desire instead of imagining it. She spent less time building futures in her head and more time noticing the texture of the life already unfolding around her. As the waiting fell away, something unexpected took its place. She began to feel connected to herself again. There was a steadiness in showing up while still afraid. A quiet trust formed, not in outcomes or plans, but in her ability to meet whatever came next. Life did not open because she finally felt ready. It opened because she stopped standing outside it.

Every time you choose today over someday, you teach yourself that your life is not on hold. Desire becomes less fragile when it is lived instead of protected. Fear loses its authority the moment movement begins. You discover that the present moment is not a threshold you must cross perfectly, but the only ground where anything real can take root. Courage is not the absence of hesitation, it's the decision to step forward with it. The life you keep imagining does not exist in some distant future. It exists here, shaped by the choices you make while uncertainty is still present. You can keep waiting for a version of yourself who feels ready, or you can let the life that wants you now begin to take form today.

16

Speak or Listen

the pattern that talks for you

The resignation letter lay between them, unavoidable in its finality. Garrett stared at Jordan's signature. The same confident scrawl that had signed grant applications and program proposals and the vision statement they wrote together seven years ago on a napkin at a diner. Something inside him cracked. Jordan, his co-founder, the person who had built half of what made this organization breathe, sat across the table with the carefully neutral expression of someone who had already stepped away. "I don't understand," Garrett said. "We just secured the Richardson grant. The youth summit you designed got picked up by three other cities. Where is this coming from?" Jordan's expression didn't change. "I've accepted a position with another organization. The approach is different. It's a better fit." Something hot rose in Garrett's chest. "Approach. Jordan, we created this approach together. We spent nights in my living room figuring out how to reach kids nobody else was reaching. We're partners."

Something flickered across Jordan's face. Not anger. Something worse. Resignation mixed with pity. "I need to be honest about something," Jordan said. "I've tried to tell you I was struggling. Multiple times over the past eight months." Garrett's stomach dropped, "What? You never said—" Jordan continued, "In March, I started to explain that the mentor matching process was burning me out. You interrupted after thirty seconds with your solution. I tried to say that wasn't the actual problem, but you'd already moved on. In July, I tried to explain why the expansion timeline concerned me. You cut me off to explain why it was necessary. Three weeks ago, I told you I was heading toward burnout. You responded with your own burnout story and tips for managing the load." Jordan's voice wavered. "You never asked what was actually causing it. Or what I needed."

Garrett's hands went numb on the table. The conversations replayed all at once. Eight months of Jordan trying to speak, and Garrett filling every opening with his own words, his own certainty about what was required, his own stories and solutions. "I wasn't trying to dismiss you," he said quietly. "I thought I was helping." "I know you did. That's what makes this hard." Jordan's expression softened, which somehow made it worse. "You genuinely care about this work, about these kids. But Garrett, you've never actually heard me. You hear the first sentence and start composing your response. You hear a problem and immediately jump to solutions. Every single conversation, I can feel you stop listening the moment you think you understand what I'm about to say." Even now, Garrett had been about to explain. To defend. To fill the space with more of his own words.

The silence between them expanded. Into it rushed every time he had cut Jordan off mid-sentence, every planning meeting where concerns had been talked over, every attempt Jordan had made to share something real that Garrett had filtered through his own framework and returned as advice. Not just with Jordan. With the program staff. With his wife. With everyone. He had been proud of his open-door approach, his quick thinking, his readiness to step in and problem-solve. He had believed those habits made him accessible. Instead, they had made him unavailable for the one thing Jordan had needed: to be heard, not advised, not fixed, not compared to Garrett's own experience. Just heard. "I'm sorry," Garrett said. "I'm so sorry I made you feel unheard in something we built together." Jordan's eyes grew bright. The careful control finally slipped, and Garrett saw the pain underneath. Years of trying to be heard by someone who was always too busy talking to listen. "Thank you for saying that," Jordan said quietly. Then they sat in silence. Garrett knew there was nothing he could say that would fix this. No solution he could offer that would change Jordan's decision. The only thing he could do, the only thing he should have been doing all along, was listen.

Why Your Choice Matters

Most of what passes for listening is simply waiting for your turn to talk. Someone begins describing a struggle, and before they finish their second sentence, your mind is already ahead of them, assembling a response, shaping advice, preparing the insight you are certain will help. You nod. You make eye contact. You offer the right sounds at the right moments. From the outside, it looks like listening. But inside, you are translating their words into your own framework, filtering their experience through your expertise, your history, your certainty. Research in communication psychology shows that most people retain only a fraction of what they hear in conversation.[50] Not because they lack intelligence or care, but because they are not actually available to receive what is being shared. They are busy preparing what comes next.

The cost of this habit is quieter than conflict but just as damaging. When people sense that you are waiting to speak rather than wanting to hear, they adjust. They simplify. They offer the manageable version of their story and keep the rest to themselves. Over time, connection thins. Carl Rogers, one of the founders of humanistic psychology, spent decades observing what happens when someone feels truly heard.[51] What he found reshaped how we understand change. Being listened to without judgment, without interruption, without advice, allows people to access insight and clarity on their own. The presence itself becomes restorative. No fixing required. No solutions offered. Your advice often protects you from discomfort. Your quiet attention serves them. Genuine listening is so rare that when people encounter it, they remember it long after the conversation ends.

Every time you interrupt someone's story with your solution, you communicate something you never intended. *I don't need to fully understand your experience because I already know what you should do.* When you listen instead, when you stay long enough to hear both what is said and what is struggling to be said, you communicate something entirely different. Your experience matters enough to be received before it is evaluated, fixed, or compared. That difference shapes everything that follows. Whether conversations deepen or remain shallow. Whether people trust you with their truth or only with what feels manageable. Whether relationships become places of genuine closeness or settle into polite exchanges of information, insight, and advice.

Why We Fill Every Second

When someone shares a problem or struggle with you, something happens before you make a deliberate choice. Your mind moves ahead of the moment, assembling responses, identifying solutions, preparing what you believe will help. This feels like engagement. Like competence. Like care. Sociologist Sherry Turkle's research on conversation in a digital age complicates this assumption.[52] She spent years interviewing students, parents, and professionals and found that we increasingly mistake constant connection and rapid response for genuine presence. Responding is *not* the same as listening. Filling space can masquerade as presence, especially in cultures that reward articulation over attention. Offering advice reassures you that you are useful, informed, participating. It allows you to remain active rather than receptive. In Turkle's work, even the presence of a silent phone on the table is enough to make people keep conversation safe and shallow, lowering empathy and the sense of being fully seen. In the moment, your brain does not clearly distinguish between listening to understand and preparing to reply. Both register as involvement. Only one allows the other person to feel fully heard.

Advice also shields you from discomfort. Sitting with someone's pain without trying to alter it demands a tolerance most people never develop. The impulse to speak is often an impulse to regulate the unease stirred up by their experience. Over time, many people learn to measure their worth in conversation by contribution rather than presence, by how quickly they can offer insight instead of how deeply they can be present. When someone brings you something tender, efficiency urges resolution. But speed comes at a cost. When you rush to respond, you teach people how to approach you. They learn to bring problems that can be handled neatly, struggles that fit your language, experiences that do not require you to stay with uncertainty alongside them. What disappears first is not drama, it's truth.

There is also a physiological dimension. Italian neurophysiologist Giacomo Rizzolatti and his colleagues in Parma identified "mirror neurons," cells that activate both when we perform an action and when we observe someone else performing a similar action.[53] Their work suggests that simply witnessing another's movements or expressions can engage some of the same neural circuits involved in doing and feeling, pointing to a built-in system for resonance and embodied understanding. Human empathy is not abstract, it's felt. When someone shares pain, your nervous system responds, creating urgency not only to relieve their discomfort, but to quiet your own. Offering solutions interrupts that shared activation. It shifts the interaction from presence into management, from alongside into above. The relief is immediate. The cost is relational. The person who learns to remain present through this activation, to stay without fixing, develops a capacity that cannot be substituted or performed. It is the capacity that makes people feel genuinely heard.

Holding the Space

Six months after Jordan left, Garrett received an email from his wife that tightened his chest. "I need to talk when you get home. Something's been weighing on me." The old Garrett would have spent the drive rehearsing responses, anticipating needs, solving problems that hadn't yet been named. Instead, he walked through the door, sat across from her, and said something unfamiliar. "I'm listening. Really listening. Whatever you need to say, I'm here." She studied him for a moment, gauging whether this was another performance. Then she began. She spoke about feeling disconnected. About missing the version of them that existed before everything became efficient. About wanting to be heard without being corrected or managed.

Garrett felt the familiar impulses rise. The urge to explain. To defend. To clarify why her perception wasn't entirely fair and how they could fix it. He noticed those impulses and let them pass. He listened for what was underneath her words rather than what he could respond to most quickly. He heard the loneliness beneath the frustration, the fear threaded through her disappointment. When she finished, he did not rush to speak. He stayed with what she had shared, letting the silence hold it. "That sounds lonely," he said finally. "I've been so focused on fixing things that I stopped being present with you." Her eyes filled. Not with sadness, but relief. "Thank you for hearing me," she whispered. That was all she had been asking for. Not solutions. Not explanations. Just the sense that her experience mattered enough to be received without being reshaped.

The shift carried into his work. The following week, when a program coordinator came to him overwhelmed by the caseload, Garrett caught himself on the edge of problem-solving. Instead, he asked a different question. "What feels most overwhelming about this?" She hesitated, then spoke for nearly ten minutes about feeling unsupported, unclear on priorities, and afraid of failing the kids they served. None of it was what Garrett would have addressed with his original plan. When the real concerns surfaced and she felt genuinely heard, solutions emerged naturally. Not forced. Not imposed. This was what Jordan had been trying to communicate all along. Not that Garrett needed to speak less, but that he needed to make room before translating someone else's experience into his own framework.

Listening required something that felt counterintuitive: treating silence not as an absence waiting to be filled, but as space where understanding can take shape. Trusting that his value was not measured by speed or insight, but by his capacity to stay present. Discovering that what people needed most from him was not expertise or answers, but attention. The willingness to remain with another person's experience without rushing to relieve his own discomfort.

When Both Options Serve the Moment

There are moments when speaking is the most loving response available. When someone is spiraling into catastrophic thinking and cannot see beyond it, perspective can steady them. When a person explicitly asks for your advice, offering it honors the request. When a child is about to make a choice that will carry real consequences, stepping in protects what still needs protection. Silence is not virtue by default. Words matter. The problem is not that you speak. It's that you have learned to speak reflexively, without discerning whether your words are serving the other person or relieving your own discomfort with quiet. Many of the situations you treat as requiring your input do not. A friend processing a relationship conflict is not asking you to solve it. A partner thinking through a career decision is not asking for analysis. A colleague naming frustration is not asking for efficiency. Calling these moments opportunities to help allows you to fix instead of feel, to advise instead of attend, to stay active rather than present.

The distinction lives in what is being asked for. Information sounds like "What would you do?" or "Do you know how to handle this?" Witness sounds like "Can I talk this through?" or "I need to say this out loud." Most people need witness far more often than they need information. When you listen first, without steering or shaping, you create conditions where clarity can emerge on its own. Only then does speaking have weight. Integration is not about withholding your voice. It's about knowing when your words deepen connection and when they merely interrupt someone else's process. The meta-skill is not conversational management. It's the capacity to trust that another person's understanding can unfold without your intervention, and that your attention, offered without agenda, is sometimes the most consequential contribution you can make.

Where This Choice Shows Up Every Day

Romantic Relationships. Your partner starts sharing something difficult about their day or their inner world. Speak moves quickly into interpretation, advice, or parallel stories meant to show understanding. Listen stays with their experience as it unfolds. It reflects what is heard without redirecting it, allowing feelings to exist without being resolved. The shift is subtle but profound. They feel accompanied rather than managed.

Parenting. Your teenager comes home overwhelmed by social tension or disappointment. Speak analyzes motives, predicts outcomes, and outlines what they should do next. Listen stays alongside the emotion long enough for it to settle. It names what is felt without rushing toward instruction, trusting that clarity develops from being heard, not from being told.

Friendship. A friend voices uncertainty about a decision that matters to them. Speak compares paths, offers preferences, or frames the choice through your own values. Listen helps them slow down enough to hear themselves. It asks what feels heavy, what feels honest, and what they are afraid to admit out loud. Often the answer was already there, waiting for room.

Professional Settings. A colleague expresses frustration with a project or role. Speak moves toward efficiency, highlighting missteps or offering immediate solutions. Listen acknowledges the complexity of the situation before addressing outcomes. It asks what support would actually help and what success would look like from their perspective, not just yours.

Family Conflicts. Old tensions surface during a gathering or a familiar wound is reopened. Speak defends, explains, or tries to smooth things over before discomfort deepens. Listen remains present with what is underneath the conflict. It resists the urge to fix the moment and instead creates space for something honest to finally be said, sometimes for the first time in years.

Practice Exercises: The LISTEN Framework

Speaking feels productive, but listening creates the conditions for real understanding. These practices help you notice when you've stopped hearing and started preparing your response, resist the urge to fill silence with solutions, and discover that your attention often matters more than your advice.

L – Let Them Finish. Notice the moment your mind jumps ahead. The impulse to respond forms before they finish the sentence. Your body leans forward. You already know what you want to say. Stay. Let them reach the end of their own thought. People often arrive at what matters most only after they think they are done speaking. When you wait, you hear what almost didn't get said.

I – Inquire Deeper. Before responding, ask one question that invites them further into their own experience. Not to gather information, but to signal that you are still with them. "What feels hardest about this?" or "What matters most right now?" Often their answer reshapes what you thought you understood. Listening deepens when curiosity replaces certainty.

S – Sit With Silence. When they stop speaking, resist the urge to fill the space. Take a breath. Let the silence hold what was shared. Silence is not absence. It gives people room to add what they were unsure how to say and gives you time to absorb meaning rather than react to it. Many conversations turn here, if you let them.

T – Test Your Understanding. Before adding your perspective, reflect back what you heard. Not the details, but the essence. "It sounds like you're feeling…" or "What I'm hearing is…" Then pause. Let them adjust or correct you. This moment matters. Until they feel accurately understood, anything you say next is likely to miss the mark.

E – Evaluate Your Urge. Before offering advice, notice why you want to speak. Is it to support them, or to relieve your own discomfort with their struggle? Sitting with someone else's uncertainty can feel tense. If your words are meant to soothe you, stay quiet. Often the most helpful response is restraint.

N – Notice the Outcome. After conversations where you listened more than you spoke, pay attention to what follows. People rarely remember the advice they were given. They remember the moments they felt received. Notice whether they seem clearer, steadier, or more at ease. Listening does not give people answers. It gives them access to their own.

The Power of Being Heard

A year after Jordan left, Garrett met him for coffee. Jordan was thriving in his new role and no longer carried the edge he once had. Garrett had changed, too. "You're different now," Jordan said. "I can tell you're actually hearing me." Garrett smiled. "I finally understood what you were trying to show me for seven years. That listening isn't passive. That presence carries weight. That the silence I offer while someone works through something difficult can matter more than any solution I could give." Jordan leaned back, considering him. "You know what I realized?" he said. "I never needed you to have all the answers. I needed you to trust that I could find mine." The words landed harder than the resignation letter ever had.

Each time you choose to listen rather than prepare to speak, you offer something most people rarely experience: to be met without being immediately improved, compared, or redirected. When you habitually fill silence with your words, you train people to bring you only what you can quickly understand and resolve. The parts of them that are still forming, conflicted, or difficult to articulate stay hidden. Over time, you become someone people consult for answers but hesitate to confide in with uncertainty.

When you learn to listen, relationships change shape. People bring more of themselves because they feel safe doing so. Trust deepens because your attention communicates respect without an agenda. You become someone people seek out not for certainty, but for space. You stop losing pieces of people to your need to be helpful, and you begin receiving something quieter and more valuable. The privilege of being trusted with thoughts that are unfinished, feelings that are still organizing, and truths that have not yet found language. Being heard is not the same as being helped. Understanding someone reaches places advice never will.

Your attention carries more influence than your expertise in the moments that define how people experience being with you. The question is not whether you have something useful to say, it's whether you are willing to wait long enough to hear what actually needs to be said. That choice appears in ordinary moments, when someone begins to speak and you feel the familiar urge to interrupt, to fix, to demonstrate what you know. You can follow it, or you can stay. Breathe. Listen. And allow the space between words to tell you what matters most.

17

Story or Truth

the fiction that feels like reality

Six days of silence, and Sarah had already attended the funeral of a friendship that wasn't dead. She sat at her kitchen table scrolling through eight years of text history with Piper, looking for the moment everything had gone wrong. They'd talked nearly every day since meeting in a pottery class in 2017. Piper knew things about Sarah that no one else knew. The time Sarah's mother was diagnosed with early-onset Alzheimer's and Sarah spent three weeks unable to tell anyone else. The miscarriage at twelve weeks that Sarah never publicly acknowledged. The truth about why her first marriage really ended. They'd planned to grow old together, two ridiculous women still making each other laugh in their eighties. Piper was supposed to be the friend who stayed.

Then six days ago, silence. Sarah's text about weekend plans went unanswered. Her follow-up the next day, the casual "you okay?" delivered, read, and ignored. Three phone calls swiped to voicemail. The Instagram story Piper posted yesterday proved she was alive and on her phone, just not responding to Sarah. Sarah's chest felt tight every time she thought about it, that familiar sensation of waiting for bad news that confirmed what she already knew. Her stomach twisted into familiar knots, the same physical response she'd had at fourteen when her best friend stopped sitting with her at lunch without explanation.

The bitter taste of rejection filled her mouth. Her hands shook slightly as she scrolled, searching for evidence of what she'd done wrong.

By day three, Sarah had constructed the first draft. Piper was upset about something Sarah said at book club last month. Sarah had laughed at a comment about people who overschedule their kids, and Piper's daughter did competitive gymnastics five days a week. That must have been it. By day four, the interpretation had expanded. Piper had been distant since Sarah couldn't make her birthday dinner in July. Sarah had apologized three times, but clearly Piper had been nursing that resentment for two months. By day five, Sarah had written the complete screenplay. Piper had decided their friendship had run its course. They'd grown apart, probably since she got engaged. The silence was intentional. Piper was doing the slow fade that hurt less than an actual conversation about how friendships sometimes end.

The pain felt real. Sarah had cried twice, drafted and deleted a long text trying to apologize for offenses she could only guess at, and told her partner that her best friendship was ending. She practiced the casual answer she'd give when people asked about Piper, "Oh, we just drifted apart, you know how it is." Then her phone buzzed. Piper calling. Sarah's hands shook as she answered, bracing for the conversation she'd been rehearsing for six days. "Sarah, thank god. I'm so sorry I've been MIA." Piper's voice was thick with exhaustion. "My dad had a heart attack Tuesday morning and I've basically been living at the hospital. He's going to be okay, but it's been completely overwhelming."

The entire elaborate explanation Sarah had constructed collapsed at once. Piper wasn't upset with her. Wasn't phasing her out. Wasn't punishing her for past failures. Piper's silence had nothing to do with Sarah at all. She'd spent six days living in complete fiction, feeling genuine grief about a problem that didn't exist while her best friend went through a crisis. She could dismiss this as reasonable misunderstanding or face something more uncomfortable. That mental movie playing in her head had nothing to do with reality, and this wasn't the first time she'd suffered deeply over narratives created entirely in her own imagination.

Why Your Choice Matters

You are not living in reality. You are living in a version you wrote about reality, and most of the time you can't tell the difference. Someone does not text back and you have written a three-act drama about why they are angry. Your boss schedules an unexpected meeting and you have already been fired in your imagination. Your partner seems quiet and you diagnose relationship problems that may not exist. A friend posts photos from a gathering you were not invited to and you construct an explanation about being excluded, unwanted, systematically rejected. These interpretations feel absolutely true while you are inside them. Your body responds as if they are facts, releasing stress hormones in response to scenarios that exist only in your mind. The distress you experience is real. The problem causing it exists only in your imagination.

Most of your pain comes not from what is happening, but from what you think is happening. The gap between these two realities is where human misery takes root. You interpret, assume, project, and narrate your way through experiences, missing what is actually occurring while carrying what you have imagined. Your mind is a meaning-making machine that never stops running. Jerome Bruner, a psychologist whose work in narrative psychology explored how humans organize experience as stories, argued that we do not simply register reality.[54] We construct narratives that explain what events mean and who we are inside them. You take fragments of reality, a facial expression, a delayed text response, a subtle change in routine, and weave them into complete explanations. This is not a flaw in your design. It is how the mind works. Your brain evolved to create coherence from incomplete information. The problem is that it does not distinguish between interpretations rooted in evidence and interpretations driven by anxiety. Both feel equally convincing. Both generate suffering that feels entirely real.

Sarah's explanation about Piper rejecting her created the same suffering as actual rejection. Six days of genuine grief about a friendship that was not ending. Six days of real pain generated by a story she had written. This is the cost of living in story instead of truth. Your interpretations of other people's behavior reveal more about your fears than about their intentions. The meaning your mind assigns to minimal information is rarely the full picture. When Sarah's mind decided Piper's silence meant she was angry, it felt like truth. When it insisted the distance proved their friendship was ending, the evidence seemed overwhelming. But truth asks quieter questions: Do I actually know why she has not responded? What evidence exists beyond my interpretation? What else might explain this silence? The person who learns to make this distinction stops confusing imagination for reality. You are not discovering truth. You are narrating a fiction and calling it reality. And that fiction quietly consumes your life.

Why We Believe What We Imagine

When you encounter ambiguous situations, your brain immediately begins constructing interpretations, creating coherent explanations from incomplete information. This system once helped your ancestors navigate complex social environments where understanding intentions and predicting behavior meant survival. Your brain learned to fill gaps quickly because waiting for complete information could be dangerous. But that same mechanism overreaches in modern environments, where context is thin and ambiguity is constant. Fritz Heider, a social psychologist whose attribution theory examines how people infer causes of behavior, described how we act like naive psychologists constantly trying to explain why others do what they do.[55] Under uncertainty, you habitually sort explanations into two categories: internal causes rooted in who a person is, and external causes shaped by the situation they are in. The pattern is predictable. You attribute others' actions to character while explaining your own behavior through circumstances. When someone does not respond to your message, you assume it reflects something about how they feel toward you rather than considering the many reasons they might be unavailable. You give yourself grace for being busy or overwhelmed, but when others behave the same way, you experience it as personal rejection.

The discomfort of uncertainty drives this pattern relentlessly. When faced with incomplete information, you will accept almost any explanation that provides closure rather than tolerate not knowing. Your mind prefers a wrong answer to no answer at all. Sarah spent six days building elaborate theories about Piper's silence instead of sitting with uncertainty. The unease of not knowing felt more difficult to hold than the imagined explanation she created. Once an interpretation takes hold, it reinforces itself. You begin searching for confirming evidence while dismissing information that contradicts it. Eight years of text history turn into a crime scene, neutral moments reread through a lens of rejection. Over time, these interpretations can become self-fulfilling. Responding from defensive hurt can create the very distance you feared in the first place.

Digital platforms intensify this pattern by removing the cues that once anchored interpretation in reality. Tone, body language, timing, and context disappear, leaving gaps your mind feels compelled to fill. Read receipts confirm a message was seen but reveal nothing about what came next. Social media offers fragments detached from the lives they belong to. In that absence, your mind steps in, not to understand, but to protect. The story you create is rarely neutral. It often bends toward threat, rejection, or loss. Not because those outcomes are most likely, but because they are the ones your nervous system knows how to prepare for. The explanation feels like control, but it quietly conditions you to live in anticipation of harm, responding to imagined danger while real life continues, unchanged, just outside the story you are telling yourself.

Investigating Your Fiction

Truth approaches your experience like a curious investigator rather than a creative screenwriter. Instead of immediately building explanations for ambiguous events, it asks what do I actually know? What am I assuming? What else might be true here? When you choose truth over automatic interpretation, you stop being a victim of your imagination and start questioning what generates your pain. Sarah learned to catch herself three weeks after the hospital incident. Her mother didn't return her evening phone call. Sarah felt the familiar tightness in her chest, the beginning of her interpretation forming. Mom's upset about our conversation yesterday. But this time, Sarah paused. *What do I actually know? Mom didn't call back tonight. That's it.* The interpretation lost its grip. She texted "Hope you're having a good evening, talk tomorrow?" Her mother responded the next morning. She'd fallen asleep at 8 p.m. after gardening. No crisis. Not upset.

Byron Katie, whose method of self-inquiry known as "The Work" examines how thoughts create suffering, offers a simple but radical way to practice this in real time.[56] Her approach rests on four questions: Is it true? Can you absolutely know it's true? How do you react when you believe that thought? Who would you be without that thought? These questions slow the rush from event to explanation. They create space between what happened and what you decided it meant. Sarah's crisis with Piper would have collapsed under this scrutiny. *Is it true Piper is rejecting me?* Maybe. *Can I absolutely know that's true?* No. *How do I react when I believe it?* I suffer for six days, review years of conversations searching for proof, withdraw emotionally, prepare for confrontation. *Who would I be without that thought?* Present, peaceful, available to help if something's actually wrong.

When you question the thoughts that compound your pain instead of believing them automatically, something shifts. You cannot suffer about an explanation you are no longer telling yourself. The emotions stirred by your interpretations are real: the racing heart and churning stomach and sleepless nights. But the interpretations themselves are optional. Truth doesn't eliminate uncertainty or make everything clear. It simply stops imagined suffering from accumulating on top of whatever is already happening. Reality, when you can bear to witness it without elaboration, is almost always more workable than the stories your anxiety creates to fill the silence.

When Both Options Serve the Moment

Interpretation itself isn't the problem. The difference lies between meaning-making that helps you stay oriented in your life and mental fiction that pulls you away from what is actually happening. Some meaning-making is necessary. When you have lived through a difficult event, understanding what it taught you helps the experience integrate rather than linger unresolved. When you are grieving, reflecting on what a relationship meant becomes part of how you carry it forward. When you are learning from mistakes, examining what happened can prevent the same patterns from repeating. What matters is time and evidence. Patterns that emerge across repeated experiences carry information. Explanations invented to account for a single ambiguous moment rarely do. When someone consistently behaves in ways that affect you, the repetition itself becomes meaningful. One unanswered text does not establish a pattern. Ten conversations where someone talks over you might.

Much interpretation, however, drifts into rumination. These are mental loops that circle familiar thoughts without movement or resolution. Rumination does not introduce new information. It rehearses imagined outcomes, fills silence with explanation, and builds narratives around things that could be clarified directly. Processing feels different. It allows experience to settle and change shape over time. The distinction between the two is subtle but consequential. Patterns grounded in repeated evidence tend to lead somewhere. Stories built from assumption tend to circle. Truth does not require you to abandon meaning-making altogether. It becomes visible when explanation replaces engagement with what is actually in front of you. The meta-skill isn't just distinguishing story from truth. It's choosing reality over the comfort of explanation, and discovering that not knowing is almost always more peaceful than the fiction you create to avoid it.

Where This Choice Shows Up Every Day

Relationship Uncertainty. Your partner comes home unusually quiet and your mind reaches back to the tension from that morning. The story forms quickly. They must be upset with you. Attention narrows. You begin preparing for distance before anything has actually happened. When the silence is met with a simple question instead of interpretation, a different picture emerges. A difficult client meeting explains the quiet. What could have turned into withdrawal returns to connection without requiring repair.

Professional Interactions. A colleague has not responded to your deadline email and meaning rushes in to fill the gap. You begin assigning motive. Maybe they are undermining you. When the situation is approached without narrative, a brief follow-up reveals the message never landed where it was meant to. The tension dissolves because it was never anchored in anything real.

Social Situations. You notice photos from a gathering you did not attend and the story arrives fully formed. You must be slipping from the group. When the missing context is allowed to surface, you learn the event was tied to a partner's work obligation. The friendships remain unchanged. Only the imagined exclusion disappears.

Parenting Moments. Your teenager answers in one-word replies at dinner and your mind accelerates toward diagnosis. You begin assembling futures that have not arrived. When the moment is met with curiosity instead of projection, a quieter truth appears. Anxiety about a test the next morning. The weight lifts as attention returns to what your child is actually carrying.

Health Anxiety. A persistent headache draws your thoughts toward worst-case scenarios. Each sensation becomes evidence. When attention returns to what is most common rather than most catastrophic, the picture shifts. Dehydration. Screen fatigue. Ordinary explanations that allow you to respond to what is present instead of bracing for what you fear.

Practice Exercises: The REALITY Check

Your mind fills gaps with stories faster than you notice it's happening. These practices help you catch the moment interpretation replaces observation, recognize when you're treating assumptions as facts, and return to what's actually known before the story takes over.

R – Recognize When You Are Writing Fiction. There is often a moment when the mind begins inventing explanations for something it does not yet understand. Words like "probably" or "must" tend to signal that you have moved away from direct observation and into interpretation. Noticing that shift matters. It marks the point where a story has begun to form in place of what is actually known.

E – Examine What's Known. What is known is often far simpler than the story suggests. What is known consists only of what can be observed without interpretation. Piper has not responded for six days is known. Piper must be angry is a conclusion. Placing these side by side creates clarity. It reveals how easily discomfort begins when the mind moves beyond what is known and fills the gap with explanation. Often the weight you are carrying belongs to the story, not the situation itself.

A – Alternative Explanations. When interpretation takes hold, it usually settles on a single explanation and defends it. Widening the frame changes the experience. Piper may be upset. She may be overwhelmed at work. She may be caring for someone who needs her. She may have lost her phone. When more than one explanation is allowed, the first story loses its certainty.

L – Listen for the Fear Beneath the Story. Every interpretation rests on a fear that is harder to name than the story itself. Sarah's belief that she was being rejected drew from older fears of being unlovable and from memories of losing people she cared about. When the fear underneath becomes visible, attention shifts from proving the story to understanding what is actually being touched.

I – Inquire Directly When Possible. Stories often grow in the absence of contact. When it is possible to ask instead of assume, speculation collapses quickly. A simple check-in can replace hours of internal analysis. The vulnerability of asking is real, but it often brings clarity more efficiently than any amount of mental decoding.

T – Time-Limit Catastrophizing. When imagination accelerates toward worst outcomes, it tends to run unchecked. Allowing it a boundary changes its grip. After a period of mental escalation, the question becomes simple: What, if anything, needs to be done right now? Often the answer is nothing. Seeing that creates enough space for the body to settle and attention to return to the present.

Y – Yield to What Is. There are moments when the most accurate stance is admitting that you do not yet know. The mind resists uncertainty and fills the gap with explanation. But uncertainty is often temporary. The discomfort of not knowing passes on its own. The suffering created by imagined explanations tends to linger much longer.

The Freedom That Rewrites Your Life

In the months after the hospital incident, Piper's father recovered and her friendship with Sarah deepened, but the larger shift was quieter. Sarah developed a different relationship with uncertainty. When Piper seemed distant, she asked instead of assuming. When text responses were slow, she stayed present rather than spiraling. When plans changed, she looked for information instead of writing narratives. She began catching herself in small moments. One evening her partner came home unusually quiet, and instead of rehearsing stories about their relationship, she asked what had happened. A difficult meeting at work explained the silence. Nothing to do with her. Nothing to do with them. Just a hard day that her old patterns would have turned into hours of imagined crisis and unnecessary suffering. The change was not dramatic. It was ordinary. And it changed how she moved through her life.

Each time you choose truth over automatic interpretation, you step out of the mental movie your mind creates and back into what is actually happening. That choice shapes more than a single moment. It determines whether you respond to the situation in front of you or to a crisis your imagination has already written. Whether your relationships are formed around who people actually are or around the versions you have constructed in your absence of information. Living inside interpretation means spending emotional energy on problems that do not exist, straining real relationships by responding to imagined slights, and missing opportunities for connection while tending grievances that were never confirmed. Decisions begin to take shape around fear rather than facts, all while feeling indistinguishable from being realistic about how the world works.

Living in reality instead of interpretation doesn't make life easier, but it does make it clearer. Relationships deepen because you are relating to people as they are, not as anxiety has recast them. Work becomes more navigable because you respond to actual feedback rather than anticipated criticism. Peace lives in the space between what happened and what you decided it meant. Reality, when you can bear to meet it without interpretation, proves less personal and more workable than your mind has insisted. The question is not whether you will ever tell stories, it's whether you will continue living inside them, suffering over fiction, or learn to pause long enough to ask what you actually know and allow truth, however incomplete, to be enough.

18

Worry or Wonder

the rehearsal that steals the show

At 3:17 a.m., Elena found herself wide awake again, her mind spinning through the same seventeen scenarios it had been rehearsing for hours. Earlier that evening, her 15-year-old son Miguel had been twenty minutes late coming home from basketball practice. Twenty minutes that launched her into a spiral she could not stop. What if he was in an accident? What if someone hurt him? What if he was experimenting with drugs like his cousin Carlos? Miguel had simply stopped at a teammate's house to work on a history project, a teenage decision he had texted her about. But Elena's mind had already constructed elaborate disaster scenarios, each one feeding the next until she was convinced her failure to track his every movement meant she was raising a child destined for tragedy.

Now, hours later, Miguel slept safely down the hall while Elena lay staring at the ceiling, her heart racing, that familiar pressure tightening across her chest. She had gotten up twice to crack his bedroom door and confirm he was breathing, standing there in the darkness watching his chest rise and fall, feeling both ridiculous and unable to stop herself. Back in bed, her mind cataloged new dangers. He could have a brain aneurysm like that teenager she had read about online. He could be depressed and hiding it. Her hands were cold despite the blankets. Her jaw ached from clenching. This was just Tuesday night in Elena's mind, where loving someone meant imagining every way you could lose them.

Elena had been carrying this weight since Miguel was born. Through sleepless nights checking that he was still breathing, through elementary school panic about bullies who mostly existed in her imagination. When Miguel mentioned wanting his driver's permit last spring, Elena could not sleep for three nights imagining highway collisions. She had pulled him from a camping trip because the forecast showed a twenty percent chance of thunderstorms. Miguel had been furious, humiliated in front of his friends. Elena had been convinced she had saved his life. Last week he had asked about going to a concert with friends. Elena's first response, "What if there's a mass shooting?" The look on Miguel's face, that mixture of frustration and pity, had haunted her ever since. She could see him pulling away, choosing what to share because certain topics would trigger her spiral. He was learning that being her son meant living inside the borders of her fear.

Something felt different about this 3 a.m. awakening. Maybe it was exhaustion finally breaking through the adrenaline. Maybe it was lying awake worrying about Miguel's safety while he slept peacefully twenty feet away. Or maybe it was her mother's words, spoken years earlier while Elena spiraled about toddler Miguel's fever. "Mija, worrying is like praying for things you don't want to happen." Elena had dismissed it then. Now, lying in the dark with her heart pounding over dangers that existed only in her imagination, she finally understood. She had been using the same mental energy that could wonder about who Miguel was becoming to rehearse tragedies that would likely never happen.

Elena stood at a crossroads that millions face when anxiety becomes a constant companion. She could continue letting worry consume her, spending her mental energy rehearsing problems that had not happened. Or she could redirect that same imaginative capacity toward something else. Wonder about who Miguel was becoming. Curiosity about how to support his growth. The choice was not about caring. It was between fear that treated uncertainty like an emergency and curiosity that could hold it without filling every gap. Between a mind trained to scan for what might go wrong and a mind willing to stay with what was real.

Why Your Choice Matters

Your mind's most powerful capability is also the one most likely to turn against you. The loop that begins with "What if" and quietly escalates into disaster rehearsal. The physical tension that tightens your chest when someone you love is late. The voice that steals sleep by cataloging everything that could go wrong tomorrow, next week, next year. Worry often feels like suffering, a relentless mental rehearsal of outcomes that have not occurred and may never occur. Because of this, anxiety is usually treated as an enemy, something to suppress, control, or eliminate. But research on anxiety offers a different understanding. Worry and excitement produce nearly identical physiological responses: increased heart rate, heightened alertness, focused attention. The body does not distinguish between them. The difference lies in how the mind interprets and directs that energy. The same neural activation that fuels worry can also fuel wonder. The same imaginative capacity that rehearses disaster can explore what has not yet been known. The same attention that scans for problems can be oriented toward discovery.

Worry is wonder directed toward threat. When you worry, imagination is recruited to rehearse what might go wrong.

When you wonder, that same imagination is used to stay curious about what is unfolding. Worry narrows attention toward danger. Wonder widens attention toward possibility. This is not about denying risk or pretending uncertainty does not exist. It is about noticing that the mental energy already being spent on anxiety does not disappear. It simply moves. Some people learn, often without realizing it, to orient that energy toward exploration rather than endless rehearsal. Anxiety does not vanish, its direction changes. Worry does not prevent difficult outcomes, it consumes attention before reality requires a response.

Why We Rehearse Disaster

When you face uncertainty about outcomes that matter to you, your brain makes a decision about where to invest mental resources. Michel Dugas, a psychologist whose research on generalized anxiety disorder examines how people respond to ambiguity, describes a pattern he calls intolerance of uncertainty, a tendency to react negatively to not knowing and to experience ambiguity itself as threatening.[57] You did not choose this pattern. It forms in environments where unpredictability carried consequences, where adults struggled to tolerate uncertainty, or where answers were demanded even when none were available. If your early experience included sudden crises or emotional volatility, your nervous system learned a simple equation. Not knowing meant danger. When uncertainty appeared, bad things followed. Over time, the mind adapted. Dugas's model suggests that when uncertainty feels intolerable, worry begins to function like a coping strategy, an attempt to scan for every possible problem in the hope that anticipating it will prevent it. This strategy drives the endless what-if scenarios, the constant checking, the mental rehearsal of disasters. You begin operating from the belief that certainty is both possible and necessary, that with enough attention ambiguity can be eliminated and safety guaranteed. But the safety never arrives. The vigilance only intensifies.

Digital life reinforces this pattern with remarkable efficiency. Weather apps extend forecasts days into the future. Parenting apps track development against population averages. GPS reveals exactly where your teenager is at any moment. Read receipts confirm a message was seen without explaining the silence that followed. Together, these tools create the impression that uncertainty is a technical problem waiting to be solved, rather than a condition of being human. But more information does not reduce anxiety. It multiplies the number of variables the mind feels responsible for monitoring. Each new data point becomes another possibility to manage, another imagined outcome to rehearse, and another opportunity for worry to expand.

Barbara Fredrickson, a psychologist whose research examines how different emotions shape cognition and behavior, reveals one of worry's most consequential costs.[58] When anxiety dominates, attention narrows. Fear and worry organize perception around threat detection, creating what she calls a narrowed thought-action repertoire. In this state, you are less able to notice opportunity, beauty, or possibility because cognitive resources are consumed by scanning for danger. Peripheral awareness contracts. Creativity dims. Curiosity recedes. By contrast, emotions associated with interest and wonder broaden attention and expand what the mind can hold. They allow you to notice what worry filters out. Worry often masquerades as care. Elena believed her constant vigilance proved she was a good mother, that parents who were not perpetually anxious must not care as much. But worry does not protect the people you love. It reduces your capacity to support them. When attention is consumed by imagined disasters, it is no longer available for connection, guidance, or enjoyment of the people right in front of you.

Asking Different Questions

Three weeks after that 3 a.m. awakening, Elena caught herself mid-spiral. Miguel had texted that he would be home late from a study group, and her mind immediately began assembling familiar scenarios: accident, drugs, bad influences. This time, instead of following the well-worn path deeper into disaster, she paused. A different question surfaced. What else could I do with this energy. The anxiety was still there, moving through her body with the same urgency. But instead of filling the uncertainty with imagined outcomes, her attention shifted. *What is Miguel actually doing right now? What would it be like to trust that he is making reasonable choices? What if this nervous energy did not have to be spent on fear?*

The shift felt awkward at first, like using a muscle she had neglected. Her mind tugged toward its habitual tracks. But Elena stayed with the questions. She began noticing Miguel's friendships, what drew him to certain people, what he seemed to be learning about himself through these late nights. She noticed something else as well. How it felt to watch him grow into someone capable of handling situations without her constant oversight. The anxiety did not disappear. It changed shape. The same intensity remained, but it no longer collapsed into catastrophe. It became attention.

This shift works because worry and wonder draw from the same mental capacity. When Elena redirected her what-if thinking away from disaster, she was not suppressing anxiety or forcing reassurance. She was allowing imagination to move in a different direction. Months later, when Miguel came home with a college acceptance letter, she recognized something quietly unsettling. She had spent years preparing for everything that could go wrong and almost none preparing for what might go right. Wonder asked different questions. Not what if he fails, but what might he grow into. Not what am I afraid will happen, but what is actually unfolding. The concern never vanished. What changed was how that concern was expressed. Her care remained. The channel it moved through did not.

When Both Options Serve the Moment

Sometimes worry does serve you. When your teenager mentions driving with a friend who has been drinking, the alarm that fires in your body reflects attentiveness, not imagination. When physical symptoms persist, concern that prompts a doctor's visit is care, not spiraling. When your partner seems withdrawn after a difficult conversation, noticing the change and checking in can be an appropriate response. The distinction is not between feeling concern and eliminating it. It lies in what the concern does next. Some concern moves toward clarity and action. Other concern never leaves rehearsal.

Concern that serves you tends to stay close to what is happening. It asks what needs attention now and takes a step that matches the situation. It gathers information, has conversations, sets limits, or seeks support. Then it pauses. Worry that does not serve you moves differently. It circles the same possibilities without resolution. It revisits questions that cannot be answered and searches for reassurance that never holds. The difference is not subtle in its effects. One brings orientation. The other consumes time, energy, and attention without changing anything.

Wonder does not remove necessary vigilance. It reduces unnecessary escalation. When Elena wondered about Miguel's growing independence instead of rehearsing disaster, she was not dismissing risk. She continued setting curfews, asking about plans, and teaching responsibility. What changed was where her attention lived. She stopped spending hours inside imagined outcomes and became more available to what was actually unfolding. Her parenting did not become looser. It became clearer. She could respond to who Miguel was rather than to who her fears suggested he might become. This is not about managing anxiety away. It is about recognizing that uncertainty is the space where growth occurs, and learning to meet that space with curiosity rather than treating it as a problem that must be solved. The meta-skill is transforming your relationship with the future itself, from a threat to predict into a possibility to explore.

Where This Choice Shows Up Every Day

Major Life Transitions. You start a new job and worry immediately begins rehearsing how you might fail. Will you keep up. Will they regret hiring you. Wonder turns toward what you will learn, the relationships that will form, the ways the role will stretch you. The uncertainty does not disappear. Your attention simply moves from rehearsing collapse to engaging what is unfolding.

Health Uncertainty. You are waiting for test results and your mind races ahead to diagnoses and treatments that have not been named. Worry fills the waiting with imagined outcomes. Wonder returns attention to what is present. How your body feels today. What support you have right now. The waiting remains, but the panic loosens.

Financial Decisions. Markets shift and worry scans for danger. Will there be enough? Did you make the wrong choices? Wonder asks different questions: What actually matters? What feels sufficient? How money is being used to support your life as it exists, not just the one you are afraid of losing. The numbers stay the same. Your relationship to them changes.

Aging Parents. A parent's health begins to decline and worry races ahead into responsibility, loss, and exhaustion. Wonder stays closer. It notices what still wants to be shared. The conversations that matter now. The presence that cannot be postponed. The future remains uncertain. The moment becomes more available.

Major Purchases. You consider buying a home and worry fixates on timing, commitment, and getting it wrong. Wonder shifts attention toward how the space will be lived in. The daily life it will hold. The choice does not become risk-free. It becomes grounded in something real rather than something imagined.

Practice Exercises: The WONDER Framework

Worry keeps you living in imagined futures while wonder brings you back to what's actually here. These practices help you catch when your mind has moved from preparation into rehearsal, redirect energy toward what you can actually influence, and discover that uncertainty doesn't require constant vigilance to be survivable.

W – What am I actually worried about? Worry rarely arrives clearly. It shows up as pressure, urgency, or a sense that something is wrong without knowing exactly what. When you slow it down, there is usually a specific fear underneath. Naming it can feel exposing. "I'm worried about everything" keeps you braced and scattered. Naming the particular fear brings it into focus. It does not resolve it, but it changes how it moves through you. What was swirling becomes something you can actually face.

O – Or is my mind rehearsing disaster? Some thoughts are oriented toward preparation. Others are simply repetition. The difference can be felt in the body and in time. If you have been circling the same concern without learning anything new or taking action, the mind is no longer solving. It is rehearsing. Seeing this clearly can be uncomfortable. It reveals how much energy has been spent without relief. But it also opens a pause, a moment where the loop loosens and attention can shift.

N – Notice the physical sensations. Worry does not stay contained in thought. It tightens the chest, locks the jaw, shortens the breath. Turning toward these sensations can feel like the opposite of what you want, especially when relief is the goal. But the body offers something the mind cannot. It tells you what is happening now, not what might happen later. Naming the sensations anchors you in the present moment, interrupting the cascade of imagined futures without requiring you to fix anything.

D – Direct energy toward what you can influence. Worry spends energy everywhere. Attention sharpens when it moves toward what is actually within reach. A conversation that needs to happen. A boundary that wants clarity. A small step that can be taken. Sometimes there is nothing to do yet. That realization is not failure. It is information. It tells you the worry has moved ahead of reality and is asking you to carry something that does not belong to this moment.

E – Explore what else might be possible. Worry narrows imagination until only danger fits inside it. Wonder gently widens the frame. It does not deny risk or promise reassurance. It simply allows more than one outcome to exist at the same time. Questions begin to change. What else could be happening? What capacity might be growing here? What remains unknown. These questions do not eliminate fear. They keep it from becoming the only voice in the room.

R – Return to this moment. Worry pulls attention forward, asking you to live in futures that have not arrived. Returning brings you back to what is here. The weight of your body. The steadiness of the floor. The simple fact that this moment is still intact. Nothing about the future is solved by this return. But something important is restored. You are no longer required to live ahead of yourself.

The Show You've Been Missing

Three years after that 3 a.m. awakening, Elena received a late-night text from Miguel. "Staying at Diego's tonight. Long story. I'm safe. Love you." Her first instinct was familiar. What's the long story? Why can't he tell me now? What if he's in trouble? But instead of reaching for her phone to demand details, she noticed the anxiety rising and paused. *What did she actually know?* Miguel had texted her. He was at a friend's house. He said he was safe and that he loved her. Everything else was projection, the same disaster groove she had spent years learning to recognize. She texted back, "Thanks for letting me know. See you tomorrow. Love you too." And then, she went to sleep.

The next morning, Miguel told her what had happened. His friend's parents had a serious fight, and his friend was overwhelmed, so Miguel stayed to support him. The long story wasn't about danger. It was about Miguel becoming exactly the person Elena had hoped he would be. Compassionate. Present. Willing to sacrifice comfort to be there for someone he cared about. If Elena had spiraled that night, demanding immediate explanations, she would have sent a different message. That his judgment could not be trusted. That safety required control. Instead, she got to listen. And when the story ended, she got to say, simply, "I'm proud of you."

This is what wonder makes possible that worry cannot. The ability to stay present with who people actually are instead of becoming consumed by who you fear they might become. The capacity to witness growth as it unfolds rather than trying to manage every struggle in advance. Worry pulls attention forward, demanding certainty before life has offered it. Wonder keeps attention closer, allowing you to notice character, values, and care taking shape in real time. The difference is not in how much you care, but in where your attention lives while you are caring.

Over time, this changes how you live with uncertainty. You become less compelled to fill every unknown with explanation. More able to remain engaged without guarantees. You learn that care does not require constant vigilance, and that love does not demand rehearsal of loss. Worry does not keep anyone safe. It keeps you braced, exhausted, and elsewhere. Wonder does something quieter. It makes room to stay with what is happening, even when you do not yet know how it will unfold.

The person who understands this shift no longer treats imagination as a warning system. They recognize it as a source of energy that can be aimed. Worry uses that energy to rehearse threats before they exist. Wonder uses it to stay attentive to what is real and emerging. One exhausts you ahead of life. The other keeps you available for it. The choice is not between certainty and risk, or vigilance and care. It is between spending your attention preparing for futures that rarely arrive, or being present for the life that is already here.

page left intentionally blank

Notes

1. Robert Waldinger and Marc Schulz, *The Good Life: Lessons from the World's Longest Scientific Study of Happiness* (Simon & Schuster, 2023); Robert Waldinger, "What Makes a Good Life? Lessons from the Longest Study on Happiness," TED Talk, January 2016, video, 12:47, https://www.youtube.com/watch?v=8KkKuTCFvzI.
2. John Bowlby, *Attachment and Loss*, vol. 1, *Attachment* (Hogarth Press, 1969); John Bowlby, *Attachment and Loss*, vol. 2, *Separation: Anxiety and Anger* (Hogarth Press, 1973); Inge Bretherton, 'The Origins of Attachment Theory: John Bowlby and Mary Ainsworth,' *Developmental Psychology* 28, no. 5 (1992): 759–775.
3. Sue Johnson, *Hold Me Tight: Seven Conversations for a Lifetime of Love* (Little, Brown, 2008); Susan M. Johnson, *The Practice of Emotionally Focused Couple Therapy: Creating Connection*, 2nd ed. (Brunner-Routledge, 2004).
4. Susan David, *Emotional Agility: Get Unstuck, Embrace Change, and Thrive in Work and Life* (Avery, 2016).

5. Dylan G. Gee, "Caregiving Influences on Emotional Learning and Regulation: Applying a Sensitive Period Model," *Current Opinion in Behavioral Sciences* 36 (2020): 177–184; Daniel J. Siegel, "An Interpersonal Neurobiology of Psychotherapy: The Developing Mind and the Resolution of Trauma," in *Healing Trauma: Attachment, Mind, Body, and Brain*, ed. Marion F. Solomon and Daniel J. Siegel (W. W. Norton, 2003), 1–56.
6. Steven C. Hayes, Kirk D. Strosahl, and Kelly G. Wilson, *Acceptance and Commitment Therapy: The Process and Practice of Mindful Change*, 2nd ed. (Guilford Press, 2012).
7. Jill Bolte Taylor, *My Stroke of Insight: A Brain Scientist's Personal Journey* (Viking, 2008).
8. Kristin D. Neff, *Self-Compassion: The Proven Power of Being Kind to Yourself* (William Morrow, 2011).
9. Martin E. P. Seligman, *Helplessness: On Depression, Development, and Death* (W. H. Freeman, 1975); Lyn Y. Abramson, Martin E. P. Seligman, and John D. Teasdale, "Learned Helplessness in Humans: Critique and Reformulation," *Journal of Abnormal Psychology* 87, no. 1 (1978): 49–74.
10. Albert Bandura, *Self-Efficacy: The Exercise of Control* (W. H. Freeman, 1997); Albert Bandura, "Self-Efficacy: Toward a Unifying Theory of Behavioral Change," *Psychological Review* 84, no. 2 (1977): 191–215.
11. Gabriele Oettingen, *Rethinking Positive Thinking: Inside the New Science of Motivation* (Current, 2014); Gabriele Oettingen, "Future Thought and Behaviour Change," *European Review of Social Psychology* 23, no. 1 (2012): 1–63.

12. Timothy D. Wilson and Daniel T. Gilbert, "Affective Forecasting: Knowing What to Want," *Current Directions in Psychological Science* 14, no. 3 (2005): 131–134; Daniel Gilbert, *Stumbling on Happiness* (Vintage, 2006).
13. Sonja Lyubomirsky, *The How of Happiness: A New Approach to Getting the Life You Want* (Penguin Press, 2007); Sonja Lyubomirsky, "Hedonic Adaptation to Positive and Negative Experiences," in *The Oxford Handbook of Stress, Health, and Coping*, ed. Susan Folkman (Oxford University Press, 2011), 200–224.
14. Leon Festinger, "A Theory of Social Comparison Processes," *Human Relations* 7, no. 2 (1954): 117–140.
15. Ellen J. Langer, "The Illusion of Control," *Journal of Personality and Social Psychology* 32, no. 2 (1975): 311–328.
16. Mary D. Salter Ainsworth, Mary C. Blehar, Everett Waters, and Sally N. Wall, *Patterns of Attachment: A Psychological Study of the Strange Situation* (Psychology Press, 2015); Inge Bretherton, 'The Origins of Attachment Theory: John Bowlby and Mary Ainsworth,' *Developmental Psychology* 28, no. 5 (1992): 759–775.
17. Angela Duckworth, *Grit: The Power of Passion and Perseverance* (Scribner, 2016); Angela L. Duckworth et al., "Grit: Perseverance and Passion for Long-Term Goals," *Journal of Personality and Social Psychology* 92, no. 6 (2007): 1087–1101.
18. The Gottman Institute, "The Four Horsemen: Criticism, Contempt, Defensiveness, and Stonewalling," accessed September 9, 2025, https://www.gottman.com/blog/the-four-horsemen-recognizing-criticism-contempt-defensiveness-and-stonewalling/.
19. Adam Grant, *Think Again: The Power of Knowing What You Don't Know* (Penguin, 2023).

20. Chris Argyris, "Teaching Smart People How to Learn," *Harvard Business Review* 69, no. 3 (1991): 99–109.
21. Sonja Lyubomirsky, *The How of Happiness* (Penguin Press, 2007); Sonja Lyubomirsky, "Why Are Some People Happier Than Others? The Role of Cognitive and Motivational Processes in Well-Being," *American Psychologist* 56, no. 3 (2001): 239–249.
22. Alfred Adler, *Social Interest: A Challenge to Mankind* (Alfred Adler Institute of Northwestern Washington, 2012); Alfred Adler, *Understanding Human Nature* (Martino Fine Books, 2010); Alfred Adler, *The Practice and Theory of Individual Psychology* (Martino Fine Books, 2011).
23. Elizabeth M. Seabrook, Margaret L. Kern, and Nikki S. Rickard, "Social Networking Sites, Depression, and Anxiety: A Systematic Review," *JMIR Mental Health* 3, no. 4 (2016): e50; Ethan Kross et al., "Facebook Use Predicts Declines in Subjective Well-Being in Young Adults," *PLoS ONE* 8, no. 8 (2013): e69841; Surbhi Nimbalkar et al., "Instagram Usage and Mental Health in Young Adults: A Quantitative Study Using DASS-21," *Annals of Neurosciences* (2024).
24. Tania Singer and Olga M. Klimecki, "Empathy and Compassion," *Current Biology* 24, no. 18 (2014): R875–R878.
25. Harriet Lerner, *The Dance of Connection: How to Talk to Someone When You're Mad, Hurt, Scared, Frustrated, Insulted, Betrayed, or Desperate* (HarperCollins, 2001).
26. Melanie Klein, "Notes on Some Schizoid Mechanisms," in *Influential Papers from the 1940s* (Routledge, 2018), 337–364.

27. Brené Brown, *Daring Greatly* (Gotham Books, 2012); Brené Brown, *Braving the Wilderness* (Random House, 2017); Brené Brown, *Dare to Lead* (Random House, 2018).
28. Carol S. Dweck, *Mindset: The New Psychology of Success* (Random House, 2006).
29. Rick Hanson, *Hardwiring Happiness* (Harmony Books, 2013).
30. Richard G. Tedeschi and Lawrence G. Calhoun, "Posttraumatic Growth: Conceptual Foundations and Empirical Evidence," *Psychological Inquiry* 15, no. 1 (2004): 1–18; Richard G. Tedeschi and Lawrence G. Calhoun, "The Posttraumatic Growth Inventory: Measuring the Positive Legacy of Trauma," *Journal of Traumatic Stress* 9, no. 3 (1996): 455–471; Richard G. Tedeschi and Lawrence G. Calhoun, "Posttraumatic Growth: A New Perspective on Psychotraumatology," *Psychiatric Times* 21, no. 4 (2004): 58–60.
31. Piers Steel, *The Procrastination Equation* (Harper Perennial, 2012).
32. B. J. Fogg, *Tiny Habits* (Houghton Mifflin Harcourt, 2019).
33. Daniel J. Levitin, *This Is Your Brain on Music* (Dutton, 2006); K. Anders Ericsson, Ralf T. Krampe, and Clemens Tesch-Römer, "The Role of Deliberate Practice in the Acquisition of Expert Performance," *Psychological Review* 100, no. 3 (1993): 363–406.
34. Donald W. Winnicott, "Ego Distortion in Terms of True and False Self," in *The Person Who Is Me* (Routledge, 2018), 7–22.
35. James F. Masterson, *The Search for the Real Self* (Free Press, 1988).

36. Erving Goffman, *The Presentation of Self in Everyday Life* (Doubleday, 1959).
37. Gloria Mark, Daniela Gudith, and Ulrich Klocke, "The Cost of Interrupted Work: More Speed and Stress," in *Proceedings of the SIGCHI Conference on Human Factors in Computing Systems* (ACM, 2008), 107–110; Gloria Mark, *Attention Span* (Hanover Square Press, 2023).
38. Adam Gazzaley and Larry D. Rosen, *The Distracted Mind* (MIT Press, 2016).
39. Mary Helen Immordino-Yang, Joanna A. Christodoulou, and Vanessa Singh, "Rest Is Not Idleness: Implications of the Brain's Default Mode for Human Development and Education," *Perspectives on Psychological Science* 7, no. 4 (2012): 352–364; Mary Helen Immordino-Yang, *Emotions, Learning, and the Brain* (W. W. Norton, 2015).
40. Viktor E. Frankl, *Man's Search for Meaning*, trans. Ilse Lasch (Beacon Press, 2006).
41. Daniel Goleman, *Emotional Intelligence: Why It Can Matter More Than IQ* (Bantam Books, 2005).
42. Naomi I. Eisenberger, "The Neural Bases of Social Pain: Evidence for Shared Representations with Physical Pain," *Biopsychosocial Science and Medicine* 74, no. 2 (2012): 126–135; Naomi I. Eisenberger and Matthew D. Lieberman, "Why Rejection Hurts: A Common Neural Alarm System for Physical and Social Pain," *Trends in Cognitive Sciences* 8, no. 7 (2004): 294–300; Amy F. T. Arnsten, "Stress Signalling Pathways That Impair Prefrontal Cortex Structure and Function," *Nature Reviews Neuroscience* 10, no. 6 (2009): 410–422.

43. Frederic Luskin, *Forgive for Good* (HarperCollins, 2002).
44. Charlotte vanOyen Witvliet, Thomas E. Ludwig, and Kelly L. Vander Laan, "Granting Forgiveness or Harboring Grudges: Implications for Emotion, Physiology, and Health," *Psychological Science* 12, no. 2 (2001): 117–123; Everett L. Worthington Jr. et al., "Forgiveness, Health, and Well-Being," *Journal of Behavioral Medicine* 30, no. 4 (2007): 291–302.
45. Steven C. Hayes, Kirk D. Strosahl, and Kelly G. Wilson, *Acceptance and Commitment Therapy* (Guilford Press, 2011); Steven C. Hayes, *A Liberated Mind* (Avery, 2019).
46. Hal E. Hershfield, "Future Self-Continuity: How Conceptions of the Future Self Transform Intertemporal Choice," *Annals of the New York Academy of Sciences* 1235, no. 1 (2011): 30–43; Hal E. Hershfield, *Your Future Self* (Little, Brown Spark, 2023).
47. Irvin D. Yalom, *Existential Psychotherapy* (Basic Books, 1980); Irvin D. Yalom, *Staring at the Sun* (Jossey-Bass, 2008).
48. Tom Pyszczynski, Pelin Kesebir, and M. Lockett, "A Terror Management Theory Perspective on Human Motivation," in *The Oxford Handbook of Human Motivation* (Oxford University Press, 2019), 67–88.
49. Robert Kegan, *The Evolving Self* (Harvard University Press, 1982); Robert Kegan, *In Over Our Heads* (Harvard University Press, 1994).
50. Owen Hargie, *Skilled Interpersonal Communication: Research, Theory and Practice* (Routledge, 2021).
51. Carl R. Rogers, "The Necessary and Sufficient Conditions of Therapeutic Personality Change," *Journal of Consulting Psychology* 21, no. 2 (1957): 95–103; Carl R. Rogers, *On Becoming a Person* (Houghton Mifflin, 1961).

52. Sherry Turkle, *Reclaiming Conversation* (Penguin, 2015).
53. Giacomo Rizzolatti and Laila Craighero, "The Mirror-Neuron System," *Annual Review of Neuroscience* 27 (2004): 169–192.
54. Jerome Bruner, *Acts of Meaning* (Harvard University Press, 1990); Jerome Bruner, "Life as Narrative," *Social Research* 54, no. 1 (1987): 11–32.
55. Fritz Heider, *The Psychology of Interpersonal Relations* (Wiley, 1958).
56. Byron Katie and Stephen Mitchell, *Loving What Is* (Three Rivers Press, 2002).
57. Michel J. Dugas et al., "Generalized Anxiety Disorder: A Preliminary Test of a Conceptual Model," *Behaviour Research and Therapy* 36, no. 2 (1998): 215–226; Michel J. Dugas and Mélanie Robichaud, *Cognitive-Behavioral Treatment for Generalized Anxiety Disorder* (Routledge, 2007)
58. Barbara L. Fredrickson, "What Good Are Positive Emotions?" *Review of General Psychology* 2, no. 3 (1998): 300–319; Barbara L. Fredrickson, "The Broaden-and-Build Theory of Positive Emotions," *Philosophical Transactions of the Royal Society B* 359, no. 1449 (2004): 1367–1377.

About the Author

Corrin Spiegel studies the decisions that do not announce themselves as important, and writes about how they change everything.

A strategist and former public-sector executive with more than two decades of leadership experience, she has navigated crisis, conflict, and change. Her doctoral research examined motivation and the psychological forces that influence commitment and departure, questions she lived long before she chose to study them.

Her work sits at the intersection of human behavior, agency, and choice. She is less interested in extraordinary achievement than in the moments when a person chooses clarity over performance and integrity over optics. She does not simply communicate ideas. She gives them architecture sturdy enough to carry.

Corrin lives in the American Midwest with her son and their adopted pets.

www.corrinspiegel.com

www.ingramcontent.com/pod-product-compliance
Lightning Source LLC
LaVergne TN
LVHW010652110826
845149LV00014B/3043
9781972328248